Doggin' Massachusetts

The 100 Best Places To Hike With Your Dog In The Bay State

DOUG GELBERT

illustrations by

ANDREW CHESWORTH

CRUDEN BAY BOOKS

There is always a new trail to look forward to...

Cruden Bay Books
PO Box 467
Montchanin, DE 19710
www.hikewithyourdog.com

International Standard Book Number 978-0-9815346-9-5

Manufactured in the United States of America

*"Dogs are our link to paradise...to sit with a dog on a hillside
on a glorious afternoon is to be back in Eden,
where doing nothing was not boring - it was peace."*
- Milan Kundera

Ahead On The Trail

Also...

Introduction

Massachusetts can be a great place to hike with your dog. Within a short drive your canine adventurer can be climbing hills that leave him panting, trotting on some of the most historic grounds in America, exploring the estates of America's wealthiest families or circling lakes for miles and never lose sight of the water.

I have selected what I consider to be the 100 best places to take your dog for an outing in Massachusetts and ranked them according to subjective criteria including the variety of hikes available, opportunities for canine swimming and pleasure of the walks. The rankings include a mix of parks that feature long walks and parks that contain short walks. Did I miss your favorite? Let us know at *www.hikewithyourdog. com*.

For dog owners it is important to realize that not all parks are open to our best trail companions (see page 13 for a list of parks that do not allow dogs). It is sometimes hard to believe but not everyone loves dogs. We are, in fact, in the minority when compared with our non-dog owning neighbors.

So when visiting a park always keep your dog under control and clean up any messes and we can all expect our great parks to remain open to our dogs. And maybe some others will see the light as well. *Remember, every time you go out with your dog you are an ambassador for all dog owners.*

Grab that leash and hit the trail - you won't be able to wipe the wag off your dog's tail!
DBG

Hiking With Your Dog

So you want to start hiking with your dog. Hiking with your dog can be a fascinating way to explore the Bay State from a canine perspective. Some things to consider:

🐾 Dog's Health

Hiking can be a wonderful preventative for any number of physical and behavioral disorders. One in every three dogs is overweight and running up trails and leaping through streams is great exercise to help keep pounds off. Hiking can also relieve boredom in a dog's routine and calm dogs prone to destructive habits. And hiking with your dog strengthens the overall owner/dog bond.

🐾 Breed of Dog

All dogs enjoy the new scents and sights of a trail. But some dogs are better suited to hiking than others. If you don't as yet have a hiking companion, select a breed that matches your interests. Do you look forward to an entire afternoon's hiking? You'll need a dog bred to keep up with such a pace, such as a retriever or a spaniel. Is a half-hour enough walking for you? It may not be for an energetic dog like a border collie. If you already have a hiking friend, tailor your plans to his abilities.

🐾 Conditioning

Just like humans, dogs need to be acclimated to the task at hand. An inactive dog cannot be expected to bounce from the easy chair in the den to complete a 3-hour hike. You must also be physically able to restrain your dog if confronted with distractions on the trail (like a scampering squirrel or a pack of joggers). Have your dog checked by a veterinarian before significantly increasing his activity level.

🐾 Weather

Hot humid summers do not do dogs any favors. With no sweat glands and only panting available to disperse body heat, dogs are much more susceptible to heat stroke than we are. Unusually rapid panting and/or a bright red tongue are signs of heat exhaustion in your pet.

Always carry enough water for your hike. Even days that don't seem too warm can cause discomfort in dark-coated dogs if the sun is shining brightly. In cold weather, short-coated breeds may require additional attention.

﹒ Trail Hazards

Dogs won't get poison ivy but they can transfer it to you. Some trails are littered with small pieces of broken glass that can slice a dog's paws. Nasty thorns can also blanket trails that we in shoes may never notice. At the beach beware of sand spurs that can often be present in scrubby, sandy areas.

﹒ Ticks

You won't be able to spend much time in the New England woods without encountering ticks. All are nasty but the deer tick - no bigger than a pin head - carries with it the spectre of Lyme disease. Lyme disease attacks a dog's joints and makes walking painful. The tick needs to be embedded in the skin to transmit Lyme disease. It takes 4-6 hours for a tick to become embedded and another 24-48 hours to transmit Lyme disease bacteria.

When hiking, walk in the middle of trails away from tall grass and bushes. And when the summer sun fades away don't stop thinking about ticks - they remain active any time the temperature is above 30 degrees. By checking your dog - and yourself - thoroughly after each walk you can help avoid Lyme disease. Ticks tend to congregate on your dog's ears, between the toes and around the neck and head.

﹒ Water

Surface water, including fast-flowing streams, is likely to be infested with a microscopic protozoa called *Giardia*, waiting to wreak havoc on a dog's intestinal system. The most common symptom is crippling diarrhea. Algae, pollutants and contaminants can all be in streams, ponds and puddles. If possible, carry fresh water for your dog on the trail - your dog can even learn to drink happily from a squirt bottle.

At the beach, cool sea water will be tempting for your dog but try to limit any drinking as much as possible. Again, have plenty of fresh water available for your dog to drink instead.

·:· Rattlesnakes and Copperheads, etc.

Rattlesnakes and their close cousins, copperheads, are not particularly aggressive animals but you should treat any venomous snake with respect and keep your distance. A rattler's colors may vary but they are recognized by the namesake rattle on the tail and a diamond-shaped head. Unless cornered or teased by humans or dogs, a rattlesnake will crawl away and avoid striking. Avoid placing your hand in unexamined rocky areas and crevasses and try and keep your dog from doing so as well. Stick to the trail and out of high grass where you can't see well. If you hear a nearby rattle, stop immediately and hold your dog back. Identify where the snake is and slowly back away.

If you or your dog is bitten, do not panic but get to a hospital or veterinarian with as little physical movement as possible. Wrap between the bite and the heart. Rattlesnakes might give "dry bites" where no poison is injected, but you should always check with a doctor after a bite even if you feel fine.

·:· Black Bears

Are you likely to see a bear while out hiking with your dog? No, it's not likely. It is, however, quite a thrill if you are fortunate enough to spot a black bear on the trail - from a distance.

Black bear attacks are incredibly rare. In the year 2000 a hiker was killed by a black bear in Great Smoky National Park and it was the first deadly bear attack in the 66-year history of America's most popular

7

national park. It was the first EVER in the southeastern United States. In all of North America only 43 black bear mauling deaths have ever been recorded (through 1999).

Most problems with black bears occur near a campground (like the above incident) where bears have learned to forage for unprotected food. On the trail bears will typically see you and leave the area. What should you do if you encounter a black bear? Experts agree on three important things:

1) Never run. A bear will outrun you, outclimb you, outswim you. Don't look like prey.
2) Never get between a female bear and a cub who may be nearby feeding.
3) Leave a bear an escape route.

If the bear is at least 15 feet away and notices you make sure you keep your dog close and calm. If a bear stands on its hind legs or comes closer it may just be trying to get a better view or smell to evaluate the situation. Wave your arms and make noise to scare the bear away. Most bears will quickly leave the area.

If you encounter a black bear at close range, stand upright and make yourself appear as large a foe as possible. Avoid direct eye contact and speak in a calm, assertive and assuring voice as you back up slowly and out of danger.

Porcupines

Porcupines are easy for a curious dog to catch and that makes them among the most dangerous animals you may meet because an embedded quill is not only painful but can cause infection if not properly removed.

Outfitting Your Dog For A Hike

These are the basics for taking your dog on a hike:

▸ **Collar**
It should not be so loose as to come off but you should be able to slide your flat hand under the collar.

▸ **Identification Tags**
Get one with your veterinarian's phone number as well.

▸ **Bandanna**
Can help distinguish him from game in hunting season.

▸ **Leash**
Leather lasts forever but if there's water in your dog's future, consider quick-drying nylon.

▸ **Water**
Carry 8 ounces for every hour of hiking.

🐾 *I want my dog to help carry water, snacks and other supplies on the trail. Where do I start?*
To select an appropriate dog pack measure your dog's girth around the rib cage. A dog pack should fit securely without hindering the dog's ability to walk normally.

🐾 *Will my dog wear a pack?*
Wearing a dog pack is no more obtrusive than wearing a collar, although some dogs will take to a pack easier than others. Introduce the pack by draping a towel over your dog's back in the house and then having your dog wear an empty pack on short walks. Progressively add some crumpled newspaper and then bits of clothing. Fill the pack with treats and reward your dog from the stash. Soon your dog will associate the dog pack with an outdoor adventure and will eagerly look forward to wearing it.

🐾 *How much weight can I put into a dog pack?*

Many dog packs are sold by weight recommendations. A healthy, well-conditioned dog can comfortably carry 25% to 33% of its body weight. Breeds prone to back problems or hip dysplasia should not wear dog packs. Consult your veterinarian before stuffing the pouches with gear.

🐾 *How does a dog wear a pack?*

The pack, typically with cargo pouches on either side, should ride as close to the shoulders as possible without limiting movement. The straps that hold the dog pack in place should be situated where they will not cause chafing.

🐾 *What are good things to put in a dog pack?*

Low density items such as food and poop bags are good choices. Ice cold bottles of water can cool your dog down on hot days. Don't put anything in a dog pack that can break. Dogs will bang the pack on rocks and trees as they wiggle through tight spots in the trail. Dogs also like to lie down in creeks and other wet spots so seal items in plastic bags. A good use for dog packs when on day hikes around Massachusetts is trail maintenance - your dog can pack out trash left by inconsiderate visitors before you.

🐾 *Are dog booties a good idea?*

Dog booties can be an asset, especially for the occasional canine hiker whose paw pads have not become toughened. In some places, there may be broken glass. Hiking boots for dogs are designed to prevent pads from cracking while trotting across rough surfaces. Used in winter, dog booties provide warmth and keep ice balls from forming between toe pads when hiking through snow.

🐾 *What should a doggie first aid kit include?*

Even when taking short hikes it is a good idea to have some basics available for emergencies:

- ▶ 4" square gauze pads
- ▶ cling type bandaging tapes
- ▶ topical wound disinfectant cream
- ▶ tweezers
- ▶ insect repellent - no reason to leave your dog unprotected against mosquitoes and yellow flies
- ▶ veterinarian's phone number

The Other End Of The Leash

Leash laws are like speed limits - everyone seems to have a private interpretation of their validity. Some dog owners never go outside with an unleashed dog; others treat the laws as suggestions or disregard them completely. It is not the purpose of this book to tell dog owners where to go to evade the leash laws or reveal the parks where rangers will look the other way at an unleashed dog. Nor is it the business of this book to preach vigilant adherence to the leash laws. Nothing written in a book is going to change people's behavior with regard to leash laws. So this will be the last time leash laws are mentioned, save occasionally when we point out the parks where dogs are welcomed off leash.

Low Impact Hiking With Your Dog

Every time you hike with your dog on the trail you are an ambassador for all dog owners. Some people you meet won't believe in your right to take a dog on the trail. Be friendly to all and make the best impression you can by practicing low impact hiking with your dog:

- Pack out everything you pack in.

- Do not leave dog scat on the trail; if you haven't brought plastic bags for poop removal bury it away from the trail and topical water sources.

- Hike only where dogs are allowed.

- Stay on the trail.

- Do not allow your dog to chase wildlife.

- Step off the trail and wait with your dog while horses and other hikers pass.

- Do not allow your dog to bark - people are enjoying the trail for serenity.

- *Have as much fun on your hike as your dog does.*

No Dogs

Before we get started on the best places to take your dog, let's get out of the way some of the trails that do not allow dogs:

Arcadia Wildlife Sanctuary
 - *Easthampton*
Ashumet Holly Wildlife
 Sanctuary - *East Falmouth*
Assabet River National Wildlife
 Refuge - *Marlboro*
Bartholomew's Cobble - *Sheffield*
Boston Harbor Islands National
 Park - *Boston*
Boston Nature Center - *Mattapan*
Broadmoor Wildlife Sanctuary
 - *Natick*
Chase Woodlands - *Dover*
Crane Wildlife Refuge - *Ipswich*
Crane Meadows Wildlife Refuge
 - *Pittsfield*
Daniel Webster Wildlife Sanctuary
 - *Marshfield*
Goose Pond Reservation - *Lee*
Great Meadows National Wildlife
 Refuge - *Sudbury*

High Ledges Wildlife Sanctuary
 - *Shelburne*
Ipswich River Wildlife Sanctuary
 - *Topsfield*
Moose Hill Wildlife Sanctuary - *Sharon*
North Hill Marsh Wildlife Sanctuary
 - *Duxbury*
Oxbow National Wildlife Refuge
 - *Harvard*
Parker River National Wildlife Refuge
 - *Newburyport*
Pleasant Valley Wildlife Sanctuary
 - *Lenox*
Stony Brook Wildlife Sanctuary
 - *Norfolk*
Tower Hill Botanic Garden - *Boylston*
Wachusett Meadow Wildlife
 Sanctuary - *Princeton*
Wachusett Reservoir - *Boylston*
Walden Pond - *Concord*
Weir River Farm - *Hingham*

O.K., not great but not too bad. Let's forget about these and move on to some of the great places where we CAN take our dogs on Massachusetts trails...

1
Mount Greylock Reservation

The Park

Mount Greylock, at 3,491 feet, is the highest point in southern New England. Known geologically as a monadnock, or isolated hill, it has long attracted attention. Jeremiah Wilbur gouged the first trail to the summit around 1800 and in 1831 students from Williams College constructed the first observatory tower that poked above the trees on the top.

Throughout the 1800s trees were removed from the slopes to power local industry and as landslides and forest fires became more frequent public conservation efforts began to stir. A cadre of 42 concerned citizens formed the Greylock Park Association in 1885 to purchase 400 acres around the summit and on June 20, 1898 the Massachusetts Legislature passed a law creating the Greylock State Reservation, the first state park in the Commonwealth.

Berkshire

Phone Number
- (413) 499-4262

Website
- www.mass.gov/dcr/parks/western/mgry.htm

Admission Fee
- Parking fee at summit only

Park Hours
- Sunrise to dusk

Directions
- *Adams*; Accessed from the north just west of North Adams on Notch Road, from the south in Lanesborough from Route 7 on North Main Street. Look for brown signs.

The Walks

At Mount Greylock you can hike longer with your dog (more than 70 miles of trails), higher with your dog (some canine hikes will gain over 2,000 feet in elevation) and see more of New England's oldest trees (200+ years old) than any place in the Commonwealth. Nascent canine hikers can drive to the summit when the auto road is open and loop around on the *Overlook Trail* and *Appalachian Trail*. This sampler covers over two miles and still delivers plenty of ups and downs to complement the famous multi-state views.

For serious canine hikers there are several long-distance options to tag the summit. One of the wildest but most scenic trails on the mountain is the Thunderbolt that picks up 2,175 feet in less than two miles. The steep, twisting route was constructed in 1934 as a ski trail and named after a famous rollercoaster at Revere Beach near Boston because both gave such an unforgettable ride. Today your dog can hike where many a past major downhill championship race was contested.

In 1844 Ralph Waldo Emerson urged his friend Henry David Thoreau to climb Mount Greylock, a place he described as "a serious mountain." Thoreau took the route that today is the *Bellows Pipe Trail*, so-called for the wind gusts that are forced through the notch, and wrote about his experiences in *A Week on the Concord and Merrimack Rivers*.

If there is one must-do major canine hike in the Berkshires it is probably The Hopper. Surrounded on three sides by steep slopes, this unique valley studded with old-growth red spruce has been designated a National Natural Landmark. An 11-mile loop includes the *Hopper Trail*, the *Mt. Prospect Trail* and the *Money Brook Trail* and tags the summits of Mt. Prospect, Mt. Williams and Greylock.

Trail Sense: There is a detailed map and the trails are signed and blazed.

Dog Friendliness
Dogs are allowed on the trails and in the campground.
Traffic
This is the trademark park in Western Massachusetts and is visited accordingly; all-terrain vehicles are prohibited.
Canine Swimming
There are plenty of streams coursing down the slopes of Mount Greylock but swimming is not a strong feature of these canine hikes.
Trail Time
A full day to a full weekend.

2
Ravenswood Park

The Park

At the age of 12 Samuel Elwell Sawyer went into trade in Gloucester, eventually parlaying a local start with a dry goods dealer into a successful career as a Boston-based international merchant. His prominence, however did not match his success. Irascible and difficult to approach, few appreciated that he had funded the town library and clock tower. He bought up many parcels of land south of town - many that were his family's ancestral lands dating to the early 1700s - and dreamed of creating a woodland park to rival anything in Boston. A fire delayed his plans but after he died in 1889 his will stipulated that a park "be laid out handsomely with drive-ways and pleasant rural walks," to be named Ravenswood, thought to be for the castle in Sir Walter Scott's The *Bride of Lammermoor*.

Essex

Phone Number
- (978) 526-8687

Website
- www.thetrustees.org/pages/357_ravenswood_park.cfm

Admission Fee
- None

Park Hours
- Sunrise to sunset

Directions
- *Gloucester*; From Route 128, take Exit 14 (Route 133) and follow east towards Gloucester for 3 miles until it dead ends into Route 127. Turn right onto Route 127 and follow for 2 miles to entrance and parking area on the right.

The Walks

There are no more becoming trails to hike with your dog in Massachusetts than those in Ravenswood Park. Wide and well-maintained, the former carriage paths will delight any level of canine hiker. Wooded throughout, the 10-mile trail system is decorated with Chevy-sized glacial erratics and rolls up and down past stands of large hemlocks. The backbone of that trail system is the historic *Old Salem Road* that was once the main conduit between Salem and Gloucester but was largely abandoned after the early 1800s.

The *Ledge Hill Trail* scrambles to an abandoned quarry and along the way your dog will catch a splendid view of Gloucester Harbor. The dominant natural feature at Ravenswood is the Great Magnolia Swamp, the northernmost stand of this showy tree in the country. Discovered in 1806, many specimens of the native Sweetbay magnolia were plundered from these woods before they were protected. When in bloom the mountain laurel and pink Lady Slippers and deep green ferns transform the property into a garden painting.

Trail Sense: There are many trail junctions and some of the trail segments can be quite lengthy so take advantage of the park map and pay attention.

Dog Friendliness

Dogs are welcome to ramble off-leash past the parking lot.

Traffic

Bikes can use some trails outside of March and April.

Canine Swimming

Dogs should be kept out of the park's water but down the street a dog itching for a swim can enjoy the Atlantic Ocean from a small sandy/ rocky beach in Stage Fort Park from September 16 to April 30.

Trail Time

Hours on tap for your dog.

For a swim in Gloucester hike your dog to Stage Fort Park below Ravenswood.

17

3
Noanet Woodlands

The Park

This land was cleared for settlement and industry early in the 19th century. Samuel Fisher, Jr. used Noanet Brook to operate a sawmill, producing lumber to raise the blossoming town of Dedham. Later, the Dover Union Iron Company installed a large rolling and slitting mill that made barrel hoops, wheel rims, nail plates, and nail rods from forged iron.

In 1923, Amelia Peabody purchased Mill Farm on Dedham Street and for the next six decades she shaped the Noanet Woodlands of today. She bequeathed the original land for the 695-acre park in 1984.

Norfolk

Phone Number
- (508) 785-0339

Website
- www.thetrustees.org/
pages/341_noanet_woodlands.
cfm

Admission Fee
- None

Park Hours
- Sunrise to sunset

Directions
- *Dover*; From Dover Center, take Dedham Street east .6 mile to Caryl Park entrance and parking on right.

The Walks

You can't get there from here. Noanet Woodlands is a paradise for trail dogs; Caryl Park doesn't allow dogs. There is no parking for Noanet Woodlands, you have to park in Caryl Park. You can't get there from here. It can be confusing to newcomers but dogs are allowed on the trail/road from the parking lot that leads into the woodlands. Alternately you can park be-

Sooner or later every canine hiker here makes their way to Noanet Peak.

hind the ballfields and enter the woodlands back there. Just don't let your dog stray off that golden path.

This is flat-out one of the best places in Massachusetts to hike with your dog. The trails are wide and paw-friendly dirt and, especially in the early going, woodchips. There may be more dogs than people in the Noanet Woodlands at any given time and leashes are as seldom seen as unhappy canine hikers.

There are 17 miles of trails packed into the park, with the most common destination being the modest 387-foot Noanet Peak. Many routes lead to the open, rocky summit with its one-way view straight into downtown Boston. Most involve only modest exertion save for a short, steep final surge to the top.

Trail Sense: Even those with a heart for exploring will want to have a map in hand in the Noanet Woodlands the first time - and you are best advised to print one ahead of time. The three main trails are blazed (red, yellow and blue) and about 40 of the main trail junctions are numbered. That much is good; but without a map it won't mean much under the expanse of trees. Also there are many, many more trail junctions that aren't marked.

Dog Friendliness
Caryl Park (the part with the tennis courts and ball fields) does not allow dogs; part of the woodlands are also Caryl Park but signs indicate when you have reached the tail-friendly confines of the Noanet Woodlands.

Traffic
Bikes are restricted to designated trails and banned completely in the muddy spring. Most of the other trailusers are likely to be walking dogs.

Canine Swimming
Not really; dogs are forbidden in the mill ponds where there are dangerous drop-offs.

Trail Time
Budget a minimum of an hour in the Noanet Woodlands since it takes a fair walk just to get into the trail system from the parking lot. Once here, your dog will want many more hours.

4
Martha's Vineyard

The Park

Human habitation is thought to have begun on Martha's Vineyard before it was an island in the time before melting glaciers raised the level of the Atlantic Ocean. Some are convinced that the Norsemen visited here around 1000 A.D. and in 1524 Italian explorer Giovanni da Verrazzano is known to have sailed by and named the island Indians called Noepe, "Louisa." Other explorers gave the island a name but its enduring moniker came in 1602 from Batholomew Gosnold, who immortalized one of his young daughters and the wild grapes that grew in abundance.

Barnstable

Phone Number
- (508) 696-7400

Website
- www.mvol.com

Admission Fee
- None

Park Hours
- Sunrise to sunset

Directions
- Martha's Vineyard is reached by ferry from Woods Hole on the southwest tip of Cape Cod at the end of Route 28.

The Walks

Just off the southern coast of Cape Cod, Martha's Vineyard is an extremely dog-friendly resort destination. For canine hikers, the Sheriff's Meadow Foundation has conserved over 2,100 acres of land in more than 100 separate parcels. From these protected lands the Foundation has created eight sanctuaries open to the public, including dogwalkers. The largest trail system is at Cedar Tree Neck Sanctuary where two miles of paw-friendly trails visit hilly woodlands, secluded ponds and a small sandy beach.

For sheer dramatic scenery on a hike with your dog, there are few spots that can rival Gay's Head with its bluff and beaches. Smack in the middle of the island Correllus State Forest occupies over 5,100 acres, managed for passive recreation, on its 15 miles of bike paths. It was created in 1908 as the "Heath Hen Reserve," in an attempt to prevent the bird's extinction. Sadly, the last heath hen (an eastern subspecies of the prairie chicken) was seen in 1932.

Trail Sense: You can find a map when you need it and the Foundation properties are well-marked.

Colonial Martha's Vineyard was a vibrant place with butter churning from its inland farms and its ports a constant whirl of activity. However, British raiders during the American Revolution torched the towns and stole 10,000 sheep and 300 head of cattle from Patriot farms. The island economy was crippled until a small congregation of Methodists staged a religious camp meeting in 1835. Within 20 years the yearly retreat was drawing more than 10,000 attendees and Martha's Vineyard was reborn as a resort destination.

The tents from the camp meeting gave way to wooden cottages in Wesleyan Grove. Today more than 300 ofthese eclectic Victorian cottages remain clustered on the circular paths behind the main streets of Oak Bluffs. You and your dog can wander through the campground, placed on the National Register of Historic Places in 1979 on the Centennial of the historic Tabernacle, that served as the centerpiece of the camp meetings.

Dog Friendliness

Dogs are welcome just about everywhere you really want to hike on Martha's Vineyard.

Traffic

Of course the summer brings crowds everywhere on the island but in the off-season this is a canine hiker's paradise. Watch for bikes.

Canine Swimming

Most of the beaches restrict dogs in the high season of summer so bring your water-loving dog after Labor Day.

Trail Time

You can easily carve out a canine hike of several hours duration.

Dogs ride for free on the ferries to Martha's Vineyard and Nantucket Island.

5
Great Brook Farm State Park

The Park

Great Brook Farm is studded with local flavor. American Indians were known to use sections of this land as sacred sites. In 1691 John Barett built one of the first cloth-pulling mills in America here. It was later joined by a sawmill and a gristmill and an iron mill. Cellar holes from the dwellings of millworkers can still be readily observed from the trails. One, a garrison where pioneers erected a stone house for protection from Indian attacks, is 15 feet deep.

In 1938 Farnham Smith bought a modest 8-acre farm here to raise Holstein cows. He slowly acquired adjoining land until he owned nearly 1,000 acres. In 1974, the land became part of the Massachusetts park system.

In 1987 Mark and Tamma Duffy leased part of the park and moved their 120-head herd of cows to Great Brook with the proviso that it operate as an interpretive farm park for the public.

Middlesex

Phone Number
- (978) 369-6312

Website
- www.mass.gov/dcr/parks/
northeast/gbfm.htm

Admission Fee
- $2 parking fee

Park Hours
- Dusk to dawn

Directions
- *Carlisle*; From Route 128 take exit 31B. Follow Route 225 west for 8 miles to the Carlisle center rotary, then turn right on Lowell Street (following the sign to Chelmsford.) The Park entrance is two miles ahead on the right. The Park Office (984 Lowell Street) is just beyond the entrance, also on the right. Make a right hand turn onto North Road. Parking area is 1/2 mile down on the left.

The Walks

Just about anything your dog's hiking heart desires is on the menu at Great Brook Farm. Is he looking to reconnect with his old farm dog ancestors? Try the *Lantern Loop* and interpretive trail around the corn and hayfields. Panting for an all-day-wear-me-out adventure? There are over 20 miles of wooded trails beyond the farm fields. Remember to toss in the *Heartbreak Ridge* above Tophet Swamp for that outing. Just after one of the most pleasant woodland strolls in eastern Massachusetts? Head down the *Pine Point Loop* around Meadow Pond. Does your dog desire a little cardio work? The twists and turns around Indian Hill are the answer.

However you craft your canine hiking day at great Brook expect roomy, well-maintained footpaths. The occasional glacial erratic helps decorate the historic, ecologically rich farmland as well.

Trail Sense: The trails, for the most part, are marked but there are many little trails and many intersections so a park map is mandatory and your best plan is to print one off the website ahead of time, if possible.

Dog Friendliness
Dogs are welcome in Great Brook Farm State Park.
Traffic
The main crush of visitors is at the Ice Cream Stand, petting zoo, barn tours, etc. The woodland trails are much less used. In the winter months the trails are groomed for cross-country skiing.
Canine Swimming
Depending on the time of year, Meadow Pond can see vegetation along its banks but it is a reliable doggie swimming hole.
Trail Time
Trips on the shorter trails can last less than an hour or you take up your dog's entire day here.

6
Notchview

The Park

The earliest inhabitants of this land were the Mohican Indians who were run off their land in Albany, New York and relocated to Stockbridge in 1664. It would be another century before English settlers filtering out of eastern Massachusetts would force the Mohicans off this land as well. Remnants of the tribe today can be found in Wisconsin.

By the end of the 19th century the 3,000 acres that would become Notchview supported 20 homesteads. In 1920, Lieutenant Colonel Arthur Budd, who earned The Distinguished Service Cross for extraordinary heroism in France in World War I, met the widowed Helen Bly in London.

Mrs. Bly lived in a 250-acre estate on Route 9 she called Helenscourt. The two married and returned to the Berkshires where they set about consolidating the local farms and building the 3,000-acre estate Notchview.

After considering leaving the property to the Commonwealth or the Epicopal Church, Colonel Budd decided to bequeath his farm to The Trustees of Reservations. He died in 1965 and the park opened to the public in 1969.

The Walks

Whatever you have in mind for hiking with your dog is on the menu at Notchview. There are more than 15 miles of paw-friendly hiking trails available. First time visitors can sample Notchview on the *Circuit Trail* that loops back through the middle of the property, ducks out of the trees for a quick view and finishes back at the Visitor Center. The 1.8-mile trail travels just

Bonus

Notchview is one of Massachusetts' premier nordic cross-country ski destinations in the winter. When the snow is on the ground you can ski on one trail with your dog - the loop south of Route 9.

There are good views from this trail shelter for your dog to enjoy.

about the entire way on a pebbly farm road that is kind to the paw. Although these hills have long supported farming most of the open land has been reforested in red spruce and northern hardwoods.

After this easy ramble you can decide how much of the large park to chew off with your dog. The highest point at Notchview is the 2,297-foot Judges Hill but the reserve elevation averages more than 2,000 feet so your dog can keep his four-paw drive in reserve for most of the day.

Across Route 9 is an excellent leg stretcher - the *Hume Brook Forest Interpretive Trail*. This loop was created in the 1970s to educate the public about multiple use management and demonstrate the basic principles of modern forestry.

Trail Sense: There are detailed information boards, a visitor center, maps, trail blazes and signs at trailheads and junctions. You shouldn't need to call the St. Bernards here.

Dog Friendliness
Colonel Budd was seldom seen on the farm without his beloved dogs - they are welcome at Notchview still.
Traffic
No bikes are allowed and there is plenty of room to spread out.
Canine Swimming
There is a beaver pond here and there but dog paddling is not a highlight of your dog's outing here.
Trail Time
A full day is possible.

7
Cape Cod National Seashore

The Park

Cape Cod, first sighted by the Pilgrims in 1620, became a national seashore in 1961, the first National Park to be purchased with federal monies. Senator John F. Kennedy co-sponsored the act that led to establishing the non-donated park. Cape Cod reigns as our most popular national seashore. Where once only fishermen and whalers came, the 40-mile stretch of sand dunes between Chatham and Provincetown at the tip of the cape attracts five million visitors a year. In addition to its sandy beaches, Cape Cod National Seashore features a number of interesting historic buildings, including the Old Harbor Lifesaving Station, five lighthouses and the Dune Shacks of Peaked Hill Bars Historic District. Dune shack living emerged in the early 20th century and was based in cottages built by coastguardsmen stationed nearby.

Barnstable

Phone Number
- (508) 771-2144

Website
- www.nps.gov/caco

Admission Fee
- Beach entrance fees are collected from late June through early September when lifeguards are on duty, and on weekends/holidays from Memorial Day to the end of September.

Park Hours
- Sunrise to sunset

Directions
- *Wellfleet*; Take Route 3 south, to the Sagamore Bridge in Bourne. Follow Route 6 eastward; most park features are off Route 6 from Eastham to Provincetown.

The Walks

Cape Cod National Seashore features 11 self-guiding nature trails - unfortunately dogs are banned from all park trails. But dogs are allowed on all non-nesting unprotected beaches year-round. Walking the beaches at Cape Cod is a special experience due to limited sight distance down the shore caused by the coastline's curvature. The effect is that of a series of private beaches as you move from beach alcove to beach alcove. In addition to Atlantic Ocean beaches backed by impressive highlands, the park extends across the cape to include bayside beaches with gentler waves for canine aquatics.

Canine hikers looking to shake the sand from shoe and paw can use one of three maintainedbicycle trails, ranging from a modest 1.6 miles to a 5.45-mile loop on the *Province Lands Trail*. There is little wheeled competition for these paths in the off-season. Harbor and grey seals can be sighted on Cape Cod beaches.

Trail Sense: Pick out a landmark where you started your canine beach hike and turn around when you're ready.

Dog Friendliness
Dogs are generally welcome year-round somewhere in the national seashore. Dogs are banned from all nature trails all the time; dogs are also not allowed on any lifeguarded beach but may pass through to unprotected areas; and signs prohibiting dogs may pop up seasonally to protect nesting shorebirds.

Traffic
Despite the seashore's popularity you will be amazed how empty the beaches get - even in the summer - when you hike away from the parking areas.

Canine Swimming
Restrict your dog's aquatic adventures to the ocean during the summer but he can play in the freshwater ponds from October 15 to May 15.

Trail Time
Your dog can pick the length of his beach time.

8
Blue Hills Reservation

The Park

The first settlers came to this area 10,000 years ago and called themselves "Massachusett," meaning "people of the hills." When European explorers set sight on the forested slopes while sailing along the coastline they named the region the Blue Hills. They logged the hillsides to build houses and barns and cleared the lowlands for crops and livestock. In 1893, the Metropolitan Parks Commission made the Blue Hills one of their first purchases for land set aside for recreation. Today, Blue Hills Reservation maintains 7,000 acres of land in the shadow of Boston for outdoor activities.

The Walks

Some 125 miles of trails visit a variety of terrains from hills and meadows to forests and wetlands, including a unique Atlantic white cedar bog. Some of the canine hiking can be quite challenging and many of the trails are strewn with rocks. Great Blue Hill, rising 635 feet above the Neponsett Valley, is the highest of the 22 hills in the Blue Hills chain. Keep your head up for sweeping views of the metropolitan area. Also keep an eye out for the diverse wildlife in the Blue Hills Reservation that is not often associated with Boston - timber rattlesnakes, coyote and otters.

The marquee hike is the 4.5-mile loop from headquarters to Great Blue Hill. Narrow and twisting, the rocky route is well-marked as it crosses three hills before the steep ascent to your final destination. The northern leg of the loop will set your dog to panting more than the southern leg so plan accordingly.

Norfolk

Phone Number
- (617) 698-1802

Website
- www.mass.gov/dcr/parks/metroboston/blue.htm

Admission Fee
- None

Park Hours
- Sunrise to sunset

Directions
- *Milton*; Take I-93 to Exit 3, Houghton's Pond. Turn right at the stop sign onto Hillside Street. Houghton's Pond is located approximately 1/4 miles on the right; continue 1/4 miles to the reservation headquarters on the left.

Ambitious canine hikers will want to tackle the *Skyline Trail* that travels across the spine of the reservation for nine miles. It is the longest of the park's routes.

Trail Sense: Most of the trails are marked but a trail map is a wise purchase for day hikes - one is on sale at park headquarters (695 Hillside Street) or the Blue Hills Trailside Museum (1904 Canton Avenue).

Eliot Tower, built during the 1930s makes an ideal resting spot after a spirited canine hike to the top of Great Blue Hill.

Dog Friendliness
Dogs are welcome in Blue Hills - a water bowl is kept for canine hikers outside the headquarters.

Traffic
Equestrians, mountain bikers and skiers can all use parts of the park but if it is solitude you seek, you will find it on some trail.

Canine Swimming
Doggie aquatics are not a big part of the hiking trails but you can seek out ponds in the park. The *Houghton Pond Yellow Loop* is an easy one-mile go around the recreation pond.

Trail Time
You don't bring your dog to Blue Hills for casual, quick hikes.

9
Weir
Hill

The Park

In 1850 the "son" in the textile manufacturer Nathaniel Stevens & Son was Moses T. Stevens. The Stevens were one of the founding families in North Andover and Moses' business acumen and astute mill purchases drove the family to ever more dizzying heights.

Along the way Stevens served in Massachusetts politics and spent a couple of terms in the United States Congress in the 1890s. He also built one of the state's grandest Victorian estates, dripping in oak and mahogany paneling, leaded stained glass windows and imported marble fireplaces.

Included in his 500-acre estate was Weir (pronounced "Wire") Hill, a protruberance overlooking Lake Cochichewick that had been grazed by livestock for generations. There were no Weirs in the Stevens family, incidentally. The name comes from the submerged wooden lairs that American Indians used to trap fish spawning in the lake waters.

Essex

Phone Number
- (978) 682-3580

Website
- www.thetrustees.org/
pages/373_weir_hill.cfm

Admission Fee
- None

Park Hours
- 8:00 a.m. to sunset, although there is no gated entrance

Directions
- *North Andover*; From I-93, take Route 125 north 7.3 miles. At traffic lights, merge left onto Route 114 west. Turn right onto Andover Street (remains Route 125) and follow for .2 miles. Turn right at traffic lights (remains Andover Street) and follow for .6 miles. (past The Stevens-Coolidge Place). Bear right at fork and continue .2 miles to intersection at Old North Andover Center. Go straight over for .1 mile and then left onto Stevens Street. Continue for .8 mile. to entrance on right. Park along the road.

The Walks

This is the Boston-area hike your water-loving dog was looking for. There is almost a mile of lakeside trail at Weir Hill so it's walk awhile, swim awhile, walk awhile, swim awhile...

30

The cattle grazing days here are a distant memory; everything is tree-covered save for an open vista atop the 305-foot drumlin that serves up some nice west-facing vistas of the Merrimack Valley a scant ten minutes from the trailhead by one route. And there are many hike variations available at Weir Hill. You can bounce up and down the hill in the reservation's interior or set your dog rolling on the dirt path that hugs the perimeter along the lakes.

There are several open landing areas by Stevens Pond and Lake Cochichewick where your dog will find easy access to excellent dog-paddling.

Trail Sense: A map can be printed from the website and may be available in the trailhead kiosk. You will need it. Nothing is marked on the trails and likely as not a promising route may dead-end at private property.

Dog Friendliness
Dogs are allowed at Weir Hill and chances are most park users will have at least one four-legged trail companion.

Traffic
There is limited parking along the street so that keeps the traffic light; horses and mountain bikes are permitted.

Canine Swimming
Canine aquatic are the main attraction for your dog at Weir Hill.

Trail Time
More than one hour.

10
Upton
State Forest

The Park

One of President Franklin Roosevelt's first acts to combat the Great Depression in 1933 was to create a Civilian Conservation Corps (CCC) putting young men to work reclaiming the land. The men would be fed, clothed, housed, trained and transported to work camps across America while being paid $30.00 a month. In May of 1935 camp was established in Upton where the CCC "boys" set out to relieve the grave danger of forest fire due to acres of slash left from clear-cut logging. Before they were finished in 1938 "Roosevelt's Tree Army" had planted over 230,000 trees and shrubs mostly red and white pine, gray birch, red maple, juniper and blueberry. The men made picnic areas with fireplaces and parking areas for cars and cut open vistas at scenic locations placing stone steps to them. In today's forest there is little evidence of these efforts but their legacy is a vibrant 2,660-acre woodland ideal for passive recreation.

Worcester

Phone Number
- (508) 435-4303

Website
- www.mass.gov/dcr/parks/northeast/uptn.htm

Admission Fee
- None

Park Hours
- Sunrise to sunset

Directions
- *Upton*; From I-495 take Exit 21 for Upton. Go 3.5 miles and turn right onto Westboro Road. The entrance road to the forest is two miles on the right.

Rocks like these at Whistling Cave have played a large part in the history of Upton State Forest.

The Walks

Upton State Forest is mostly a hiking and horseback-riding park across six miles of truck trails carved by the CCC. The three-mile *Loop Road/Park Road* loop is one of the most pleasant hours you can spend with your dog in Massachusetts. The wide dirt roads roll through a shady, mixed forest leading to Dean Pond, ideally situated at the half-way point. The easy access for a doggie dip will entice even the most apprehensive trail dog in the water.

As amiable as this ramble throught Upton is, don't neglect the narrow footpaths that explore the interior of the loop. The ridges and valleys of the *Whistling Cave Trail* serve up a wilder feel than the park roads. Here you'll discover glacial erratics and a touch of challenging terrain for your canine hiker.

Trail Sense: Everything is well-marked and easy to follow in Upton State Forest. Of course if you are of a mind to explore, turn off down an unmapped footpath.

Dog Friendliness

Dogs are welcome to trot these trails.

Traffic

This is not a heavily used park. Bikes and horses are allowed but the trails are not challenging enough to get the juices of mountain bikers flowing; expect a horse or two, however.

Canine Swimming

Dean Pond is one of the best places in Massachusetts for dog paddling.

Trail Time

Once you set off with your dog you will need to spend at least an hour to complete a loop; a half-day will polish off all the trails in the forest if that is your dog's wont.

11
Tyringham Cobble

The Park

A cobble, the term is thought to derive from the German word *kobel* meaning rocks - is a rounded, rocky hill formed of bedrock, not glacial debris. In the case of Tyringham Cobble, geologist Daniel Clark discovered in 1895 that the rocks on the top of the knoll were older than those strewn around the bottom. He concluded that the cobble had broken off a nearby mountain and flipped over during a great geological cataclysm 500 million years ago.

Pioneer farmers cleared most of the Cobble by the 1760s. Members of the Shakers owned an extensive 2,000-acre farm in Tyringham by 1840 where they pastured cattle and sheep. The last of the frustrated Shakers, tired of trying to grind money out of the rocky soil, had sold out and moved to other communities by the end of the century.

Berkshire

Phone Number
- (413) 298-3239

Website
- www.thetrustees.org/pages/370_tyringham_cobble.cfm

Admission Fee
- None

Park Hours
- Sunrise to sunset

Directions
- *Tyringham*; From Route 20 turn west onto Route 102 West (towards Stockbridge) and then immediately turn left onto Tyringham Road. Follow into Tyringham and turn right onto Jerusalem Road. Entrance and parking are on the right.

In the 1930s a conservation group calling themselves "The Cobblers" purchased much of this land to thwart a proposed ski run. In 1961, their leader Olivia Cutting James died and left her part of the Cobble to the Trustees of Reservations with an expressed wish that the surviving tenants do the same. And so they did in 1963.

The Walks

Hiking the two-mile loop trail, with its blend of open-fields and mixed hardwoods, on Tryringham Cobble is one of the best hours you can spend with your dog in the Berkshires. Your exploration begins in an open field where

*Sharing the trail with free-ranging cattle is an
everyday occurrence on Tyringham Cobble.*

cattle graze as they have for 200 years. Then comes a fairly rigorous climb to summit where you'll enjoy sweeping views of a quintessential New England valleyscape.

Rather than race back down the slopes the trail juts back into the hill to join the *Appalachian Trail* for a spell and views in the opposite direction. As you drop down the Cobble along a fenced pasture don't let the distracting views take all your attention off of the slippery cowpies that mine the path.

Trail Sense: There is a basic map and information board at the trailhead; the trail is marked on the Cobble.

Dog Friendliness
Dogs are welcome to hike at Tyringham Cobble.
Traffic
No bikes are allowed.
Canine Swimming
None.
Trail Time
About one hour.

12
Mount Tom
State Reservation

The Park

The story goes that Mount Tom takes its name from Rowland Thomas, a surveyor in the 1660s who named the peak after himself. Wouldn't you? At the same time his fellow surveyor working on the opposite side of the Connecticut River, Elizur Holyoke, immortalized his name on Mount Holyoke.

Mount Tom is the southernmost and highest of the Mt. Tom Range that was forged of volcanic traprock. An early quarry extracted rock from the slopes and the flywheels of a stone crusher can still be seen in the park.

The Mount Tom Hotel was constructed on the summit in 1897, but it burned down three years later. Up it went again but it burned again in 1929 and that was it. A trolley park operated on the east side of the mountain and 600-foot downhill ski runs were carved here but today the recreation in the Reservation is mostly passive.

Hampden

Phone Number
- (413) 534-1186

Website
- www.mass.gov/dcr/parks/central/mtom.htm

Admission Fee
- None

Park Hours
- Sunrise to sunset

Directions
- *Holyoke*; entrance on Route 5 off I-91, south off Exit 18 and north off Exit 17A.

The Walks

The star canine hike on Mount Tom is the two-mile trip across the ridgeline on a chunk of the 119-mile *Metacomet-Monadnock Trail* (M&M) that runs from Connecticut to New Hampshire. The destination is the 1,202-foot summit at the southern end of the Reservation, although scenic highlights will come on the iron-tinged basaltic cliffs en route. There are variations you can execute on the 20-mile trail system but this is mostly an out-and-back excursion.

Goat Peak and its scintillating views to the north can be tackled with a loop hike including the *Beau Bridges Trail* with its septet of wooden plank crossings over energetic Cascade Brook. Don't let the west-facing panorama of the Berkshires and the Connecticut Valley make you miss the lookout tower can't be seen from the trail. It is at the end of the road behind the opening.

There are no casual hikes for your dog at Mount Tom. Even the *Nature Trail*, normally a leg-stretcher in most parks, demands a steep climb to complete.

Trail Sense: The trails are blazed and the map is reliable but there are unmarked paths out there so pay attention.

The open grate steps and open railings will keep your dog on the ground at the lookout tower atop Goat Peak.

Dog Friendliness
Mount Tom is a tail-friendly park.
Traffic
The deeper you penetrate into the mountain the fewer trail users you will meet but this is a popular destination.
Canine Swimming
Cascade Brook will serve up a refreshing sit or splash for your dog but the only animals swimming will be fish; Lake Bray is a must for water-loving dogs in the off-season.
Trail Time
Many hours possible at Mount Tom.

13
Appleton Farms and Grass Rides

The Park

Established in 1638 as a land grant to Thomas Appleton, Appleton Farms lays claim to being the oldest continuously operating farm in the United States. Nine generations later, operations include community-supported agriculture, a retail feed and mulch haying operation, and livestock and dairy programs that include White Park and Jersey cows.

The Walks

The grass rides are generous carriage paths designed by the Appletons for the pleasure of family and friends who enjoyed horseback riding. Like a wagon wheel, five "rides," as they are called in England, converge on a central clearing called the "Roundpoint."
Today the rides are mostly wooded (the real grass covers the Appleton Farms trails next door that are reserved for horses) and under paw is mostly dirt, not grass. It won't dampen your dog's enjoyment here one whit, however.

All told there are some five miles of tightly connected "rides" in the park awaiting your dog after a country lane ramble from the parking lot. The land moves gradually uphill, rising above surrounding wetlands, but never so seriously to keep these trails from providing excellent cross-country skiing in the winter.

Trail Sense: The trails aren't marked but an accurate map of the property is available to tame the confusing network of carriage paths and foot trails. The property is neatly contained by railroads tracks and roadways so you can't get lost. Not really lost, at any rate.

Essex
Phone Number - (978) 356-5728
Website - www.thetrustees.org/ pages/250_appleton_farms_ grass_rides.cfm
Admission Fee - Yes, $3 for non-members
Park Hours - Sunrise to sunset
Directions - *Hamilton*; From Route 128, take Exit 20A and follow Route 1A north for 4.5 miles. Turn left onto Cutler Road and follow for 2.2 miles. At the intersection with Highland Street, turn right. The parking area is on the right.

This granite pinnacle on Pigeon Hill once adorned the fabled Gore Hall library on the Harvard College campus.

Dog Friendliness

This is a popular destination for dog-walkers, so much so that specific guidelines have been created; in brief, no dogs are allowed in the neighboring Appleton Farms.

Traffic

Bikes are allowed in the Grass Rides but not horses.

Canine Swimming

Nope; terra firma only.

Trail Time

More than an hour available.

Northfield Mountain

The Park

FirstLight Power Resources operates and maintains recreational facilities available to the public at the Northfield Mountain Station, one of its 14 power-generating sites in Massachusetts and Connecticut. The facility at Northfield produces electricity through pumped storage. During periods of lower electrical power demand, the plant pumps water from this lower reservoir to a man-made upper reservoir. At times of high demand water is released to flow downhill from this upper reservoir through a turbine generator, where it collects in the lower reservoir to be stored until again pumped to the upper reservoir.

Franklin

Phone Number
- (800) 859-2960

Website
- www.firstlightpower.com/northfield/

Admission Fee
- None

Park Hours
- 8:00 a.m. to sunset

Directions
- *Northfield*; on Route 63, two miles north of Route 2.

When the Northfield Mountain pumped-storage hydroelectric plant went into commercial service in 1972, it was the largest facility of its kind in the world. So where is the plant? It was built entirely underground.

The Walks

The Northfield Mountain trail system is one of the best maintained (the trails won't open for hiking until they are well past the squishy stage) and well-marked trails to bring your dog in Massachusetts. With 25 miles of trails fanning out up the mountain from the parking lot, you can craft any type of canine hiking day.

For an easy sampler, try the one-mile *Nature Trail*. Most long-distance dogs will eventually make their way to Rose Ledge, a 60-foot high cliff with views over the undulating treetops. The hemlocks and hardwoods are dense enough that your dog won't even see the massive gneiss wall until she is standing beneath it if approaching on the *Lower Ledge Trail*. The round trip, including a return across the top of Rose Ledge will take about an hour.

Trail Sense: Some of the narrow trails are not always obvious - if you can't trust your dog's nose, make sure you score a detailed color map from the kiosk in front of the Visitor Center.

Dog Friendliness
Dogs are excluded from the trails during ski season.

Traffic
Mountain bikes are allowed on the trails and horses are too but this is not a heavily visited park.

Canine Swimming
Unfortunately, water is not a feature of such an extensive trail system.

Trail Time
A half-day and more is possible.

15
Sandy Neck

The Park

Sandy Neck is a six-mile long barrier beach at the bottom of the bowl of Cape Cod Bay that shelters a richly diverse salt marsh and Barnstable Harbor. It is rigorously managed by the Town of Barnstable to balance public use with the preservation of the natural environment.

The first Cape settlers set livestock free in Sandy Neck to graze on tasty salt cordgrasses until an ordinance was enacted to protect the remaining vegetation. In 1715 Sandy Neck was set aside as a "reserve" for residents of the town to establish fishing houses so when shore whaling was a major local industry, Sandy Neck was the site of try works for the processing of whale blubber. Today the only signs of civilization on Sandy Neck are historic hunting shacks that dot the edge of the marsh.

Barnstable

Phone Number
- (508) 362-8300

Website
- www.town.barnstable.ma.us

Admission Fee
- limited free parking for trails

Park Hours
- 8:00 a.m. to 9:00 p.m.

Directions
- *West Barnstable*; From Route 6 follow Route 149 north to Route 6A. Turn left and go three miles to Sandy Neck Road and turn right. Continue to the gatehouse at the end of the road.

The Walks

The trail system at Sandy Neck is essentially a simple grid with the *Beach Access Trail* and *Marsh Trail* both running the length of the sand spit and tied together by a pawful of numbered connector trails. Thus you can choose the length of your canine hiking loop. For those dogs seeking to only sample Sandy Neck, the first crossover at *Trail #1* is a little less than a half-mile down the beach, creating a loop back through the primary and secondary dunes that can be completed in around an hour. The *Marsh Trail* return ducks into a maritime forest where red cedar, black cherry, sassafras and pitch pine battle the salt-laden winds. The full tour of 12 miles will consume the better part of six hours.

The beach at Sandy Neck is cobble-studded sand that may be awkward for your dog to walk on but it will be easier than slogging through the soft sand of the vehicle ruts. If possible, time your arrival to hike the beach at low tide that will provide access to the hard sand below the waterline. It will also lessen the impact of any tidal streams cutting across the beach. While you are consulting tidal charts also take note of any recent coastal flooding.

Hiking with your dog at Sandy Neck is best done in the cooler months which works out well since dogs are not permitted in the beach park (that contains the main parking lot) from May 15 to September 15. The trails are only a few blocks from downtown West Barnstable so you could walk in from there if you have a way to park on the resident streets. The cool weather will also obviate protective measures against salt mosquitoes and biting green flies.

Trail Sense: There are brochures provided by the town available online and on-site; the trail junctions are signed. Don't go looking for *Trail #3* - it has been discontinued and returned to nature.

Dog Friendliness
Dogs can go unleashed on Sandy Neck until March 1.
Traffic
Off-road vehicles along the beach; horses too. In the off-season the only other prints in the sand you are likely to see will be your dog's.
Canine Swimming
Six miles of Cape Cod Bay shoreline awaits with gentle surf that should not intimidate any water-loving dog.
Trail Time
At least one hour and up to a full day of canine hiking.

16
Mount Washington State Forest

The Park

In the late 1600s Robert Livingston married into the wealthy Van Rennselear family of New York and soon parsed together an empire of 175,000 acres from the Hudson River eastward. In 1705 he swallowed large chunks of the Berkshires under the Patent of Westenhook. By this time a handful of Dutch families were already living in this area.

English settlers began arriving to live on land granted as free towns by the Massachusetts Colonial Legislature. Livingston charged rent to these newcomers and tempers flared, culminating in the killing of William Race by a group of Livingston's agents in 1755.

When forty proprietors purchased a plantation on Taghconic Mountain (Mount Washington) in 1757, Livingston's agents burned six farms. It took 17 years to resettle the area and the Town of Mount Washington was finally incorporated in 1779.

Berkshire

Phone Number
- (413) 528-0330

Website
- www.mass.gov/dcr/parks/western/wnds.htm

Admission Fee
- None

Park Hours
- Sunrise to sunset

Directions
- *Mount Washington*; From Route 7 south of Great Barrington take Route 23/41 West for 4.9 miles to South Egremont. Turn left onto Route 41 South, then take the immediate right onto Mount Washington Road. Continue as it becomes East Street. The parking area is at Forest Headquarters on the right.

The Walks

The marquee canine hike in Mount Washington State Forest is the 2.8-mile trek to Alander Mountain and its expansive 270-degree views. You'll be going down as much as up for most of the early going but after a double stream crossing it is straight up to the 2240-foot peak. Until the campground about halfway to the summit the going is on a wide jeep road and there will be plenty of unbridged stream crossings that your dog will happily bound through. You will finish on a traditional, rock-studded, often wet footpath.

This bridge will get your dog across Ashley Hill Brook on the Alander Mountain Trail.

When your dog gets his fill of mountaintop views of the Hudson Valley and the Catskills you can return by the same route or continue across to the *South Taconic Trail.* Heading south, you'll reach the tops of Mt. Brace and Mt. Frissell and close your full-day loop in the state forest on the *Ashley Hill Trail.*

If you just want to walk your dog in the woods it is also possible to wander the trails without climbing the mountains on shorter loops.

Trail Sense: An information board with maps is at the trailhead. The trails are blazed and a distance/direction sign pops up every now and then.

Dog Friendliness
Dogs are allowed throughout the park.

Traffic
Alander Mountain is a popular destination and all trails below the campground are multi-use.

Canine Swimming
The streams are mostly for splashing only.

Trail Time
At least three hours to reach Alander Mountain and return; up to a full day to include other peaks.

17
Whitney and Thayer Woods

The Park

Henry Melville Whitney was a man of vision. He used over a million of his dollars built in the shipping business to buy large tracts of land along Beacon Street in Brookline. Here he developed one of the poshest suburbs in the United States to which he lured Bostonians with his newly built rail line, the West End Street Railway. His little single-line track soon had 2,000 horse-drawn streetcars and soon he was head of Boston's entire trolley system.

Henry Whitney loved horses; he even owned a horseshoe company. And it is quite likely this man of vision had no taste for what he saw coming after 1900 - the horseless carriage. In 1904 the 65-year old Whitney began assembling parcels of land to create a private estate in Cohasset for his equestrian pursuits. He built a magnificent mansion and carved carriage roads for horse-drawn buggies and bridle trails for riders on 600 acres of land known as Whitney Woods.

The land was donated to the Trustees of Reservations in 1943 and an adjoining parcel to the west was eventually added from Mrs. Ezra Ripley Thayer, wife of a one-time dean of the Harvard Law School, to form today's park.

The Walks

As you might expect from a park created for horseback riding, there are very long trails here and this is a super spot to bring your dog for that multi-hour adventure. The paths are also wide, well-maintained, a pleasure for your dog to trot on. If you put in the full tour you will eventually reach

Turkey Hill, from whose 187-foot summit there are spectacular views of Cohasset Harbor and the South Shore.

But you needn't spend a whole day here either; there are short-hike options. If you come in the spring or early summer one stretch of trail you will want to take extra time to reach is the _Milliken Memorial Path_ that was planted with showy azaleas and rhodedendrons in the 1920s by a loving husband.

The wooded landscape here is notable for its abundance of glacial erratics. Here Rooster Rock is supported only by its tiny neighbor.

Trail Sense: There are far fewer side trails off the main chutes in Whitney and Thayer Woods than are found in some reservation lands. The junctions are well-marked and the map easy to follow.

Dog Friendliness
Dogs are permitted to ramble under voice control here and in the neighboring Turkey Hill. The fun ends for your canine hiker - no dogs in adjacent Weir River Farm.

Traffic
Light - and it's a big place so count on long pieces of solitude.

Canine Swimming
Canine hikers only on this trip.

Trail Time
Many hours possible.

18
Borderland
State Park

The Park

When she graduated as president of Smith College, Blanche Ames said in her commencement address, "We are fortunate to live in an age that—more than any other—makes it possible for women to attain the best and truest development in life." That address was delivered not in 1999 or 1979 but in 1899 when women could not even vote. An ardent suffragist, Ames fulfilled her prophecy as a celebrated artist and author; she even invented a device to ensnare low-flying aircraft in World War II.

In 1900 she married Oates Ames - unrelated - whose grandfather helped build the Transcontinental Railroad. Six years later the couple moved here, consolidating failing farms on property that once supported mills and an ironworks, naming the country estate "Borderland." Blanche Ames died in 1969 and two years later the property began its tranformation into a park.

Bristol

Phone Number
- (508) 238-6566

Website
- www.mass.gov/dcr/parks/borderland

Admission Fee
- $2.00 parking fee

Park Hours
- 8:00 a.m. to sunset

Directions
- *North Easton*; From I-95 take Exit 10 and turn left at the end of the ramp and follow this road three miles to the traffic lights in Sharon Center. Continue straight and bear right onto Pond Street for 1-1/2 miles until the traffic rotary. Go onto Massapoag Avenue for three miles to the park entrance on the left.

The Walks

When you bring your dog to Borderland it will be like visiting the Ames estate 100 years ago. Enjoy an easy hike on the wide, flat carriage road that has morphed into the 3-mile *Pond Walk*. Short detours lead to the remnants of a white cedar swamp and an aromatic pine grove.

For more spirited canine hiking head into the narrow, twisting trails behind the Visitor Center and north of Leach Pond. The woodlands here are studded with granite outcroppings from the rocks embedded in the trails to house-

-sized boulders. Rarely will your dog have a level paw-fall on the miles of loops here. It will be no surprise to discover an old quarry along the trail.

Trail Sense: The trails are named and signed at junctions but not all the little trails are marked on the map. If you sample much of the 20 miles of trail here there is a good chance you wind up on a trail you weren't expecting - especially when a trail leads across the back of a bare rock outcropping.

Ames Mansion is the anchor of the 1,570-acre Borderland State Park.

Dog Friendliness
Dogs are welcome to trot the park, just like the Ames' dog Fuzz did many years ago; poop bags are provided.

Traffic
Count on encountering trail users from mountain bikes to equestrians, especially around Leach Pond.

Canine Swimming
There are six ponds scattered across Borderland State Park.

Trail Time
It will be hard to spend less than one hour here with your dog.

19
Stockbridge Trails

The Park

Nathaniel Hawthorne called the Ice Glen, a cleft in the rocks between Bear and Little mountains, "the most curious fissure in all Berkshire." It is a ravine without a stream - all the water around Ice Glen flows on a south-north axis while the gorge is aligned east to west. In fact, the dry Glen, stuffed with stacked boulders and draped with hemlocks, was once a glacial lake. Tucked away from the sun's rays, the season's last snow clings here, hence its name.

The Laurel Hill Association, America's first village improvement society, was started by Mary G. Hopkins in Stckbridge in 1853. The organization maintains the trails, including the 1936 stone suspension bridge over the Housatonic River that replaced the original 1895 span.

Berkshire

Phone Number
- None

Website
- None

Admission Fee
- None

Park Hours
- Sunrise to sunset

Directions
- *Stockbridge*; From the center of Stockbridge at Routes 102 and 7, turn left onto Route 7 and go two blocks. Before the bridge, turn left onto Park Road and follow two blocks to the end.

The Walks

The canine hiking begins across that bridge with a set of three completely different trails. An easy warm-up for your dog is the *Mary Flynn Trail*, a wide, flat packed-gravel path along the Housatonic River built mostly on the bed of the old Berkshire Street Railway trolley line - America's first trolley car was built in Stockbridge in 1880. The trail was constructed in 2003 as part of the Laurel Hill Association's 150th Anniversary celebration.

Across the railroad tracks the trail chugs uphill into the woods, heading for a split. To the left will be a short, switchbacking climb of 600 feet- steep enough to get your dog panting. The destination, a bit less than one mile away, is Laura's Rest, where a 35-step tower in a clearing provides views of three states.

Laura was the daughter-in-law of David Field, the donor of the land back in 1891. After losing her husband and children the young woman often came up here for solace. The trail does continue over the mountain for three miles to Beartown State Forest if you so choose.

The marquee trail in Stockbridge bears right from that junction, into the Ice Glen. The elevation gain is minimal but the boulders that litter the floor of the ravine

The chokestones in the Ice Glen ravine make for one of the most unusual canine hikes your dog will ever find.

may inhibit some dogs from going through the narrow fissure - only one-quarter-mile long. If your dog can't complete the entire trail she can still enjoy some of New England's largest pine and hemlock trees.

Trail Sense: There is a basic map and information board at the trailhead; the trails are not enthusiastically blazed but that's not a problem.

Dog Friendliness
Dogs are allowed on these trails behind the village of Stockbridge.

Traffic
The park is open to foot traffic only - no vehicles.

Canine Swimming
The Housatonic River can serve a doggie swimming pool for a determined dog-paddler.

Trail Time
Several hours to complete the trio of canine hikes here.

20
Maudslay State Park

The Park

Frederick Strong Moseley was the eighth in descent from John Maudesley - or Moseley - who came to this country as early as 1630 from Lancashire to settle in Dorchester. The son of a ship-builder and banker, Moseley hired Martha Brookes Hutcheson, one of America's earliest female landscape architects to design an estate on ancient agricultrual grounds along the bluffs of the Merrimack River in 1904. William G. Rantoul was retained to design a lavish 72-room mansion house. He called his 450-acre estate Maudesleigh and its fame was spread in magazine articles and books.

The mansion was demolished in 1955 and a second large house burned to the ground in 1978. In 1985 the Commonwealth of Massachusetts acquired the property and today only a few of some 30 structures remain from the glory days of Maudesleigh.

Essex

Phone Number
- (978) 465-7223

Website
- www.mass.gov/dcr/parks/northeast/maud.htm

Admission Fee
- $2 parking fee

Park Hours
- 8:00 a.m. to sunset

Directions
- *Newburyport*; Take Exit 57 from I-95 onto Route 113 east for half a mile and turn left on Noble Street. At the stop sign turn left onto Ferry Road and bear left at fork and follow signs (pay attention) to park.

The Walks

There is truly a feel of walking your dog on a country estate in Maudslay State Park. Most of the explorations take place on easy-going farm paths and carriage roads under woodlands that retain their sense of orderliness derived from the landscaped origins. Rhododendrons, azaleas, and lilacs are peppered throughout the understory. The mountain laurel is one of the largest naturally occurring stands in Massachusetts and the tall pines may never have been harvested.

The scenery moves swiftly from riverside views to deep pine woods to open meadows – with lots of hidden spots once reserved for the rich and famous. Around any corner you might find an obscured garden or a shingled barn or remnant of a great iron gate.

The terrain is gently rolling but Castle Hill aways off in the northeast part of the park can set doggie tongues to panting. But not too much.

The small pet cemetery has been well maintained on the estate for 75 years.

Trail Sense: There is a map available but a better way to bring your dog to Maudslay is with the intention to poke around an old estate. Walk down a path that isn't on the map. Try that little walkway that seems overgrown. And so on.

Dog Friendliness

Dogs are welcome in the state park - the dog-loving Moseleys would have had it no other way.

Traffic

This is a busy park; everyone from joggers to equestrians to strollers seeking out a picnic spot. The further you push away from the mansion site towards Castle Hill the fewer trail users you will encounter. But if you are looking for a communal dogwalk, this is a good choice.

Canine Swimming

This is not a water-loving dog's paradise.

Trail Time

Pick your outing; you can keep it short or stretch it out with your dog in one of Massachusetts' most beguiling parks.

21
Pittsfield
State Forest

The Park

George Washington made a land grant here in 1777 to William Berry in exchange for his service at the Battle of Bennington in the Revolutionary War. Over the years, like most mountains in the Berkshires the trees began to fall - first for grazing fields and cropland, then for iron blast furnaces and, eventually by 1900, for the Estes Stave Factory to manufacture wooden caskets.

Much of what you find in Pittsfield State forest today is complements of the Civilian Conservation Corps during its stay in the 1930s. They built roads, dams and many of the present-day buildings. Most noticeably hundreds of acres of spruce and red pine were planted that give the park its leafy appearance today.

The Walks

There are over 30 miles of mostly multi-use trails criss-crossing Pittsfield State Forest - and at times it can feel like

Berkshire

Phone Number
- (413) 442-8992

Website
- www.mass.gov/dcr/parks/western/pitt.htm

Admission Fee
- Parking fee in season

Park Hours
- Sunrise until 8:00 p.m.

Directions
- *Pittsfield*; Take Route 7 to Route 20 West. Turn right on to Hungerford Avenue, continue for .2 mile, then bear left onto Fort Hill Avenue, and continue for 1 mile. Turn left onto West Street. Continue for .2 mile, and turn right onto Churchill Street, and continue for 1.7 miles to Cascade Street. Turn left and follow the brown lead-in signs to the park.

there are twice that many. The focal point for most day visitors will be around the Berry Pond Circuit Road. Berry Pond, on the shoulders of the ridgeline of the Taconic range, is Massachusetts' highest natural body of water at 2,150 feet in elevation. Of the several routes to its shores, the yellow-blazed *Honwee Loop Trail* segment nearest the paved road is probably the easiest for your dog to scale Berry Mountain. Vehicles are barred from the trails around the Circuit Road - the further you branch out the more you bring your dog into contact with the four-wheelers.

A postcard from 1913 shows how open the land in Pittsfield State Forest was before a spirited flurry of reforestation created today's appearance.

At Berry Pond you can access the *Taconic Crest Trail* that travels for 35 miles through the undeveloped mountains. Both New York and Massachusetts in 1993 recognized the Taconics, a nearly unbroken wilderness, as a significant biological, scenic and timber-producing resource.

Trail Sense: The trails are blazed and a two-side map, for summer and winter use, is available.

Dog Friendliness
Dogs are allowed on the trails and in the campground.
Traffic
These are well-frequented trails, including use by four-wheelers. In late spring, when the woods are aflame with wild azaleas, Pittsfield State Forest is a busy place.
Canine Swimming
The ponds are few and far-between; refreshing energetic streams are a prime feature of canine hiking in the day-use area.
Trail Time
Many, many hours available.

22
Mount Watatic

The Park

Mt. Watatic is thought to have been the home of Wituomanit, the deity who guarded the Algonquin Indian households from misfortune. The Algonquins frequently made pilgrimages to the summit of the dome-shaped mountain that in profile resembles a traditional wigwam. The mountain's name comes from the Algonquin word "witeoauk" meaning "wigwam place."

European settlers did not attribute similar sacred properties to Mt. Watatic. The mountain was logged and turned into pastureland so the only pilgrims for 100 years were cattle. In 1964 the mountain was developed as

Middlesex

Phone Number
- (978) 597-8802

Website
- www.mass.gov/dcr/steward-ship/rmp/rmp-mtWatatic.htm

Admission Fee
- None

Park Hours
- Sunrise to sunset

Directions
- *Ashby*; Go 4.9 miles west of Ashby Center on Route 119 to parking area on the right.

a convenient ski resort for Bostonians. Competition from higher mountains and a lack of snow melted the ski business by 1984 and Mt. Watatic rested for a bit until new developers planned a large cell phone tower on the summit and a housing subdivision at the base. This proposed abomination spurred local preservation groups to raise an astounding $900,000 to save 700 acres of once sacred land in 2002.

The Walks

The expansive summit of 1,832-foot Mt. Watatic is not wooded, unusual for such a low elevation. It actually resembles a mountain top three times as high. The classic 270-degree sweep of the Mt. Watatic views and its proximity to Boston make this one of the most popular hikes in Massachusetts.

The mountain lies at the junction of two long-distance trails: the *Wapack Trail* to the north and the *Mid-State Trail* to the south. Most canine hikers will want to skip these multi-day hikes and settle for the two-hour round trip to tag the summit. The journey begins along an abandoned country lane, the old

Nutting Hill Road that was built in 1752. Turn right on the yellow-blazed _Wapack Trail_ and begin the honest climb up the mountain; suitable for any dog with only a few steep pulls on the otherwise moderate trek.

After soaking in the sights on the summit, a side path leads 400 feet southeast over the ledge to the lower southeast peak, affording more fine views. You can return down the same foot trail or extend your dog's time on the mountain by looping on the trail that bows out to the north.

The open summit is the main attraction of Mount Watatic.

Trail Sense: The trails are well-marked and well-trod but finding a map to have it all make sense may be difficult; newcomers will probably meet someone to assuage any unpleasant confusion.

Dog Friendliness
Dogs are welcome to join the fun on Mt. Watatic.

Traffic
Count on company besides your dog just about any time of the year.

Canine Swimming
Nope, not here, although a small stream can be refreshing.

Trail Time
Two hours minimum to several days possible.

23
Arnold Arboretum

The Park

When the Father of Landscape Architecture, Frederick Law Olmsted created Boston's fabled Emerald Necklace of six parks in 1880 he wrote of the Arboretum site, "On (these) acres much the best arboretum in the world can be formed."

The Arboretum was founded in 1872 when the President and Fellows of Harvard College became trustees of a portion of the estate of James Arnold, a New Bedford whaler in the early 1800s.

Botany professor Charles Sprague Sargent collected thousands of plant specimens and carefully sited them by their genus, or common family. Olmsted laid out the road system and overall planting scheme to make it blend naturally with the other parks in the Necklace.

Today Boston's tree museum spreads across 265 acres where more than 15,000 trees, shrubs and vines grow under the careful eye of the Arboretum's plant stewards.

Suffolk

Phone Number
- (617) 524-1718

Website
- www.arboretum.harvard.edu

Admission Fee
- None

Park Hours
- Sunrise to sunset

Directions
- *Boston*; Take Route 93 south or Route 1 south to Storrow Drive west to the Kenmore Square/ Fenway Route 1 south exit. Bear left. Follow signs for Fenway/Route 1 south. Bear right onto Boylston Street, following signs for Boylston Street Outbound/Riverway Route 1. Continue on Boylston for .4 miles as it turns into Brookline Avenue. After 1/2 mile turn left onto the Riverway/Jamaicaway to a rotary at Jamaica Pond. Follow signs for South Dedham/Providence. Enter the next rotary and take the second exit onto Route 203 east. The main entrance is about 50 yards past the rotary, on the right.

The Walks

There is no prettier hike you can take with your dog in Massachusetts than at Arnold Arboretum. The paths curve gently across the property and before you know it your dog has reached the top of Peters Hill with one of the city's best vistas playing out before him among the gingkos and honey locust trees. Or peering through the lilac collection at the city skyline on Bussey Hill.

You can easily spend your dog's hiking day just strolling the historic roadways but tree enthusiasts will want to test the natural surface paths. And don't restrict your explorations to just the marked paths - walk your dog into the collections to get a thorough arboreal education.

Trail Sense: Maps of the arboretum are available to lead you to the world-class collections that are more than a century old.

Dog Friendliness
Leashed dogs are welcome in Arnold Arboretum.
Traffic
The arboretum is a delight any time of year; your dog will love it just as much when the leaves are down and so are the crowds.
Canine Swimming
The ponds and streams are for decoration, not canine aquatics.
Trail Time
More than an hour, especially if you study the plants.

24
Stevens Glen

The Park

It can be hard to picture but this remote spot, as wild as any place in the Berkshires, was once one of the busiest tourist destinations in the the county. The Stevens family owned the Glen since 1760 and in 1884 Romanza Stevens built bridges and staircases to the Glen and waterfall. He charged 25 cents for tourists to view the magic of Lenox Mountain Brook.

Later a dance pavilion was added and hundreds of people would come to Stevens Glen to party. In 1919 heavy snows collapsed the roof of the dance hall and after that the property reverted to obscurity for 70 years as trolley lines bypassed the Glen.

In 1995, brothers Millard and Frederic Pryor donated the Glen and 128 surrounding acres to the Berkshire Natural Resources Council. BNRC built footbridges and a new trail that was dedicated in 1998.

Berkshire

Phone Number
- (413) 499-0596

Website
- www.bnrc.net/TrailMaps/
StevensGlenGuide.pdf

Admission Fee
- None

Hours
- Sunrise to sundown

Directions
- *West Stockbridge*; From the center of Lenox, take Route 183 South for 1.5 miles. When Route 183 bears left, go right on Richmond-Lenox Road. After 1.6 miles turn left onto Lenox Branch Road. After about 1/2 mile look for a small sign for the Glen and a pull-off on the side of the road. Overflow parking is available further down the road.

The Walks

A short flight of steps leads to this delightful canine hike, a loop of some 1.2 miles with a spur leading to the Glen itself. The trail is a topsy-turvy affair with sweeping ups and downs across energetic streams and through an airy hemlock and mixed hardwood forest There is enough elevation change as the route twists through the trees to provide any dog with a worthy workout.

The spur trail drops down and climbs back up, building a sense of mystery as it climbs to the dark, hidden Glen. A platform hanging over the 100-foot sluice of water crashing through a narrow gorge is reached by a set of metal steps that may cause your dog to think twice before descending.

Trail Sense: The trail is reliably blazed with red markers.

Dog Friendliness
Dogs can hike to the secluded Glen.
Traffic
Foot traffic only and very little of it.
Canine Swimming
The streams are deep enough only for a refreshing splash.
Trail Time
About one hour.

25
Savoy Mountain State Forest

The Park

Savoy Mountain State Forest is located atop the Hoosac Mountain Range, an extension of the Green Mountains of Vermont, and is the first mountain barrier encountered rising west of the Connecticut River Valley. "Hoosac" is an Algonquin word meaning, place of stones.

Settlement of the remote towns of Florida and Savoy by farmers began in the early 19th century. The construction of the Hoosac Tunnel (1851-75) for railroad transportation created a momentary population boom. But after its completion the tunnel workers left. Many moved down in the valley to Adams or North Adams to work in the woolen mills, or headed west to join in the great land rush for better farmland. Savoy Mountain State Forest was created in 1918 with the purchase of 1,000 acres of abandoned farmland following this exodus.

Berkshire

Phone Number
- (413) 663-8469

Website
- www.mass.gov/dcr/parks/western/svym.htm

Admission Fee
- Yes, parking fee in season

Park Hours
- 8:00 a.m. to dusk

Directions
- *Florida*; From downtown North Adams follow Route 2 East for five miles. Turn right onto Central Shaft Road, .4 miles from the Florida town line. Keep right at the next two forks, continuing to stay on Central Shaft Road. From Route 2 the park headquarters is 2.8 miles, North Pond day-use area is 3.3 miles, and the campground is 3.7 miles.

The Walks

There is plenty to set tails to wagging in Savoy Mountain State Forest. For dogs who like to tag mountain summits the high point is Spruce Hill at 2,566 feet, purchased with a relatively benign climb of 600 feet along the *Busby Trail*. Views are to the south across the Hoosac plateau and to Mount Greylock. Borden Mountain tops out at 2,500 feet - your dog won't get much of a view here but if the tower is open you can get above the treetops.

For water-loving dogs the plunges, cascades and slides that adorn Ross Brook and Parker Brook are highlights in the central area of the forest. The star of these drops is Tannery Falls, a 75-foot series of large plunges and major cascades where the upper 35-feet is a constant whirl of whitewater, even in times of low flow.

Savoy Mountain State is liberally latticed with old fire roads - you can park and hike with your dog for distance or drive up close to the major attractions.

Trail Sense: Trail maps are available that come in handy when stumbling across an unblazed trail.

Dog Friendliness
Dogs are allowed throughout Savoy Mountain Forest and in the campground (but not the cabins).

Traffic
Off-road vehicles are not allowed; most of the trails are multi-use.

Canine Swimming
In addition to the lively streams there are several major ponds in the forest for the swimming dog in your family to enjoy.

Trail Time
Completely up to you - depending on how long your dog wants to trot.

26
Halibut Point
State Park

The Park

The name Hailbut Point comes not from the fish but from early mariners who had to tack around the mass of granite on the Cape Ann shoreline, a procedure known as "haul about." Those sheets of granite are 440 million years old and in the 1800s blocks of Cape Ann rock were prized around the country as street pavers and building stone. Quarrying commenced on a small scale in 1824 when a Mr. Bates arrived from Quincy and leased a ledge for that purpose. At its height the Rockport Granite Company employed 800 quarry workers. The Cape Ann granite industry collapsed in the 1920s as streets began to be paved in asphalt and buildings were made from steel. The company went out of business and its Babson Farm quarry here closed in 1929. Today, a single granite quarry remains in operation on Cape Ann.

Essex

Phone Number
- (978) 546-2997

Website
- www.mass.gov/dcr/parks/northeast/halb.htm

Admission Fee
- $2 parking fee

Park Hours
- 8:00 a.m. 8:00 p.m., Memorial Day to Labor Day; sunrise to sunset the rest of the year

Directions
- *Rockport*; Exit I-95 onto Route 128 north toward Gloucester and Rockport. After crossing the Annisquam River bridge, go three quarters around the first rotary, following signs for Route 127 north (Annisquam and Pigeon Cove). After approximately 6 miles, turn left at the park sign and the Old Farm Inn onto Gott Avenue.

The Walks

There are actually three parks here shoulder-by-shoulder to bring your dog. Halibut Point State Park is the best for hiking with a compact trail system that features a self-guided walking tour around the Babson Farm Quarry that is now filled with 60 feet of water. The dirt trail is wide and easy to navigate with your dog but keep her leashed as the edges are not fenced and the drop-offs are long and sheer. A short detour leads to a scenic overview atop a mountain of waste granite pieces that were dumped on the edge of the sea for many decades.

Adjoining the state park to the east is Halibut Point Reservation and next to that is the Sea Rocks owned by the Town of Rockport. The hiking here is mostly functional, a way to get your dog down to the tidepools in the Atlantic Ocean. Eye-high vegetation may obscure your destination much of the way but the free-form rock hopping and salt spray will set your curious dog's tail to wagging here.

The waves break over your dog from every direction in the tidepools at Halibut Point.

Trail Sense: Things can get confusing once you venture off the self-guided quarry trail but the parks cover a small enough area that your dog won't need to dial 9-1-1.

Dog Friendliness

Dogs are welcome in all three parks.

Traffic

Foot traffic only here and you should have no trouble finding a private tidepool for just your dog.

Canine Swimming

Water play, absolutely. But the shallow, wave-battered tidepools don't lend themselves to dog paddling. That tempting blue water in the quarry is off-limits, however.

Trail Time

Less than an hour of hiking but plenty of playtime in the tidepools or lounging on the sunny Cape Ann rocks.

27
Mt. Holyoke Range State Park

The Park

The Mt. Holyoke Range formed some 200 million years ago when lava flowed from the valley floor, cooled and was upended. More recently, glaciers left their signature, scouring the ridge's jagged edges smooth in some places, exposing bedrock, or depositing till, sand, clay or muck in others. Since early days, settlers used all but the sheerest inclines for woodlots and pastures.

The unique east-west oriented ridge is now totally wooded; parcels acquired by the state since the 1970s have built the park to over 3,000 acres.

Hampshire

Phone Number
- (413) 586-0350

Website
- www.mass.gov/dcr/parks/central/hksp.htm

Admission Fee
- None

Park Hours
- Sunrise to sunset

Directions
- *Amherst*; Notch Visitor Center is on Route 116 south of town.

The Walks

Parking lots at the four cardinal points permit attacking the Mount Holyoke Range with your dog from any direction. Most assaults are planned from the east or west and work across the ridge on one of two long-distance trails, the white-blazed *Metacomet-Monadnock Trail* (M-M) or the orange-blazed *Robert Frost Trail*. These two actually share the same path for much of the journey but if you are executing a one-way canine hike with a car shuttle, dog owners are advised to take the *Robert Frost Trail* to avoid the boulder scramble at the Horse Caves that are suitable only for an athletic dog.

This ridge hike serves up its share of ups and downs but much of the way the travel is anything but strenuous. Don't expect dramatic views popping up along the way - Rattlesnake Knob that offers a northern view and an eastern exposure will be the finest - but enjoy a long woods walk with your dog.

Looking to tackle the Mount Holyoke Range by forging up the flanks? Take your pick of forest types to climb through. The southern slope supports oak and hickory forests like those of lower latitudes. The northern face favors hemlock, white pine, birch, beech, and maple.

Trail Sense: There are more than 30 miles of marked trails here. Things are easy enough to follow and signs point the way at key junctions but many routes overlap so pay attention.

Dog Friendliness
Dogs are allowed throughout the park.
Traffic
You will have no trouble finding hours of solitude on the Mount Holyoke Range, especially off the ridge.
Canine Swimming
Streams are few and far between and not deep enough for swimming.
Trail Time
A full day of canine hiking is possible.

Your dog may have trouble figuring out a way around the Horse Caves.

28
Leominster
State Forest

The Park

In the early 1700s, a series of land grants were given to the heirs of soldiers killed in battle by the General Court of Massachusetts Bay Colony. Many of these parcels became part of the unincorporated settlement known as Notown, almost all of which is part of Leominster State Forest today. In 1838 the lands of Notown were finally incorporated into the towns of Leominster, Fitchburg, Westminster and Princeton.

Frontier conflicts led to the area's most famous incident when Mary White Rowlandson was released from captivity on May 2, 1676 after having been taken prisoner three months earlier in a raid by 400 Nipmucs, Narragansetts, and Wampanoags. Her bible was a source of comfort throughout, and her sewing skills, quickly discovered, placed her in good favor; for a shilling, she was asked to make a shirt for King Philip, great sachem of the tribes. The exchange for ransom took place on a flat-topped outcrop overlooking a meadow now known as Redemption Rock. She wrote about her ordeal and it became a 17th-century bestseller on both sides of the Atlantic with 15 editions published before 1800.

Worcester
Phone Number - (978) 874-2303
Website - www.mass.gov/dcr/parks/central/lmsf.htm
Admission Fee - None
Park Hours - Sunrise to sunset
Directions - *Westminster*; Take Route 2 to Route 31 and turn south. The main parking areas are on the left.

The Walks

Your dog can count on a sporty outing in Leominster State Forest. *Ball Hill Trail*, that pushes out from the main parking lot is one of the tougher climbs in the park. Come in early summer and the explosion of white mountain laurel blooms will make the uphills go down that much easier. The trip to Rocky Pond along the *Rocky Pond Trail* will be a must-do for any water-loving dog.

Across Route 31 the Crow Hills and *Midstate Trail* are the marquee attractions for day hikers. The scenic ridgeline crosses the Crow Hill Ledges that should be saved for an athletic dog with nearly vertical climbs on either end. Dogs without nerve can make it but expect to have to help out with a lift going up or down.

The trails further out in the 4,300-acre forest are designed and maintained by local mountain bike associations if your dog hasn't gotten enough of these rollicking trails.

Trail Sense: You can count on the trail maps found at the parking lots to get you around the forest; the major trails are blazed.

Even if your dog doesn't want to join in the rock-climbing fun at the Ledges, she can still watch others scale the cliffs.

Dog Friendliness
Dogs are welcome to trot the wooded trails here.

Traffic
Hikers may be the minority at Leominster behind the lake swimmers, rock climbers and mountain bikers. Horses are allowed; off-road vehicles are not.

Canine Swimming
When the beach closes the lakes and ponds in the park are a paradise for dog paddlers.

Trail Time
Plan on at least an hour for any outing with your dog here.

29
Blackstone River and Canal Heritage State Park

The Park

The success of the Erie Canal in the 1820s set politicians and businessmen across the East to dreaming. In Central Massachusetts that dream was to link the textile manufacturers of the the Blackstone River, "the Birthplace of the Industrial Revolution," with the Atlantic Ocean via Providence, Rhode Island. Between 1828 and 1848, segments of the river were paralleled by a canal on which barges, pulled by a team of two horses, carried freight and passengers. Top speed on the Blackstone Canal was three mph and the 44-mile journey usually took two days to complete. Initially highly successful, the canal was made obsolete by the completion of the railroad in 1847. In 1986 the Blackstone River Valley was designated as a National Heritage Corridor by the United States Congress.

Worcester

Phone Number
- (508) 278-7604

Website
- www.mass.gov/dcr/parks/central/blst.htm

Admission Fee
- None

Park Hours
- Sunrise to sunset

Directions
- *Uxbridge*; From Route 146 take the Uxbridge Exit for Route 16 and travel east for 2 miles. Turn left (north) on Route 122, go 1-1/4 miles and turn right onto Hartford Avenue. In 1 mile, turn right on Oak Street and continue to the Visitor Center.

The Walks

One of the easiest and most historic hikes you can take with your dog is along the three miles or so of preserved towpath beside the Blackstone River. There are a dozen interpretive sites along the way. From the Visitor Center north to Plummer's Landing is a bit under two miles and passes the Goat Hill Lock; a loop hike back can also be executed from Goat Hill. On the east side of the river the *King Phillip Trail* winds to Lookout Rock that was used as a lookout post during the King Phillip War by the Wampanoag Indians. Today that post surrenders a splendid views of the Blackstone River and the surrounding countryside.

Millville Lock is the only intact lock of the 48 that allowed canal boats to climb or descend the 438 feet of altitude change on the way from Worcester to Providence. These locks were constructed with large stones from the Farnum quarry, owned by the architect of the locks. The stones were delivered on rafts all along the River. Though the wooden gates that raised and lowered the water are long gone, the large slabs of granite remain as they were built in 1825-6. The Millville Lock is reached on a 3/4-mile hike down an abandoned railroad bed off Route 122, six miles south of Heritage Park in the town of Millville. Beyond the Lock is a triad of rusted, abandoned railroad structures that were never finished as two competing railroads each failed rather than collaborating to get their lines across the river.

To the south, the towpath leads to the Stanley Woolen Mill. The owners of the Stanley Mill purchased water rights from the defunct Blackstone Canal Company and converted the canal into a trench to supply water to power the mill. The Stanley Woolen Mill produced wool fabric from 1853 to 1987, supplying cloth for soliders' uniforms for every American conflict from the Civil War through Viet Nam.

The Blackstone River runs wild through high rocks at Blackstone Gorge about 6 miles south through Millville into Blackstone (turn right on County Road, following signs to the gorge). The short, scenic trails are located left of Roaring Dam.

Trail Sense: There are plenty of maps and interpretive signs to help guide you to the various attractions spread out along the canal.

Dog Friendliness
Dogs are welcome to explore the heart of the Blackstone Valley.

Traffic
Expect to encounter other trail users most of the year on the *Towpath Trail*; bikes and horses are permitted as well.

Canine Swimming
Absolutely. You will find access points for your dog in the Blackstone River.

Trail Time
At least one hour to experience this historic water route.

30
Lowell Holly
Reservation

The Park

Lowell Holly is not a person and it is not a type of tree but rather a blend of both. The person is Abott Lawrence Lowell, president of Harvard University from 1909 to 1933, and donor of this 135-acre peninsula between two ponds. The tree is the American Holly, thriving here at the northern fringe of its natural range. Wilfred Wheeler, a former Massachusetts Secretary of Agriculture and an enthusiastic member of the American Holly Society, planted some fifty varieties of American holly during his stint as the first reservation director.

The Wampanoags called this Grinch-head of land "Kumunut," meaning beach, and that is the main reason your dog will love this place.

Barnstable

Phone Number
- (508) 679-2115

Website
- www.thetrustees.org/pages/316_lowell_holly.cfm

Admission Fee
- None

Park Hours
- Sunrise to sunset

Directions
- *Sandwich*; From Route 6, take Exit 2 onto Route 130 south and follow for 1.5 miles. Turn left onto Cotuit Road and follow for 3.4 miles. Then turn right onto South Sandwich Road and follow for .6 miles to the entrance and parking area on the right.

The Walks

There are four miles of gently rolling cart roads and footpaths that link the highlights of the reservation that include long views across the large ponds from isolated points of land and ornamental plantings of mountain laurel and catawba rhododendrons. The white blossoms of the rhododendrons spice up canine hikes here into August.

But all this is likely to be lost on a water-loving dog. Lowell Holly features two small sand beaches; each offering a different swimming experience for your dog. The placid waters and sandy bottom of Conaumet Cove in Wakeby Pond may lure even the most water-averse dog in for a swim. For more spirited canine aquatics walk across the thin neck of sandy soil and let your dog jump into the wind-churned waters of Mashpee Pond.

Trail Sense: One look at the park map should suffice.

Dog Friendliness
If you come to Lowell Holly without a dog in tow you will feel out of place. Dogs are not permitted on the swimming beach on Wakeby Pond next door.

Traffic
Foot traffic only; this is not a crowded park but it is small.

Canine Swimming
This is one of the best places in Massachusetts for your dog to swim.

Trail Time
About one hour.

Dogs aren't the only ones who enjoy the swimming in Mashpee Pond.

31
Monument Mountain Reservation

The Park

The "monument" of Monument Mountain was a distinctive pile of stones at the base of its southern slope that inspired myriad Mohican Indian legends and tickled the muse of artists as early as 1815. William Cullen Bryant composed "Monument Mountain," an episodic poem that recounted one Mohican tale of doomed forbidden love.

Others were not so romantic. Treasure hunters had scattered the rock pile by the middle of the 19th century and Monument Mountain supported farming and iron smelting activities that devastated the woods until stands of red pine were planted in the 1930s to reforest the landscape.

Berkshire

Phone Number
- (413) 298-3239

Website
- www.thetrustees.org/
pages/325_monument_
mountain.cfm

Admission Fee
- None

Park Hours
- Sunrise to sunset

Directions
- *Great Barrington*; Parking for the recognizable landmark is on the west side of Route 7, north of Great Barrington and south of Stockbridge.

In 1877, after most of the farms were abandoned, David Dudley Field Jr. built a scenic drive on the mountain for public use. In 1899, Helen Butler, daughter of a prominent New York attorney acquired many of the old farmlands and donated them to the Trustees of Reservations.

The Walks

Thanks to a loop trail that approaches the summit from two directions, there are several options for hiking with your dog at Monument Mountain. If you are after a spirited workout take off on the *Hickey Trail* from the north end of the parking lot. After a short circle around the base of the mountain you will begin pulling straight up beside a splendid seasonal waterfall. For a longer, but less intensive climb, use the *Indian Monument Trail*, the remnants of the 1877 carriage road that gradually works up the western slopes.

The two trails merge just below the summit at Inscription Rock, memorial-

The most famous story about Monument Mountain took place on August 5, 1850 when Nathaniel Hawthorne, having just finished The Scarlet Letter and the leading American literary figure of the day, met a young novelist named Herman Melville on a hike here.

The two men were part of a party, including Oliver Wendell Holmes, who hauled a wagon loaded with picnic food and wine up the mountain. Rain started pelting the slopes and the men took refuge in a cave to begin a friendship that led Melville to call at Hawthorne's Lenox cabin a few days later.

He eventually moved to Pittsfield where he completed the novel the two men had been discussing - Moby Dick. Melville dedicated the book, published in 1851, to Hawthorne. Their friendship, however, was fleeting. Hawthorne moved his family back to the Boston area a year later and the two writers only met once more.

Take care in bringing your dog up to Squaw Peak.

izing the gift of the property. The 1,642-foot trail high-point and the celebrated views from Squaw Peak are reached on a rocky scramble along the *Squaw Peak Trail*. Unless your dog is in no way skitterish do not bring her to the summit - there are rock climbs and unguarded, precipitous drop-offs. It is certainly doable, but the exposed cliffs of Monument Mountain are not the place to test an inexperienced trail dog.

Trail Sense: Everything is in place to prevent you from getting lost on the mountain.

Dog Friendliness
Dogs are allowed to climb historic Monument Mountain.

Traffic
This can be quite a communal hike during prime times of the year. No bikes are allowed but hunting is permitted.

Canine Swimming
None.

Trail Time
The complete loop to the top of Monument Mountain covers three miles and will take between 90 minutes and two hours.

32
Bradley Palmer State Park

The Park

Ten thousand years ago the Wisconsin Glacier formed these low hills, eskers and outwash plains. As the glacier moved, the stones and debris it dragged along wore away much of the land surface. It is a common New England tale.

By 1834 D. Thomas Manning had an industrial complex operating here on the Ipswich River that included a woolen mill, boarding house and factory. Fifty years later it burned to the ground and industry never took hold again.

In the early 1900s Bradley Palmer, a wealthy lawyer and industrialist most known as the attorney for Sinclair Oil during the Warren Harding administration's Teapot Dome scandal, bought this land. He bought a lot of land on the North Shore - at one point he owned over 10,000 acres. In 1923, Bradley Palmer gave the Hood Pond section of Willowdale State Forest to the Commonwealth of Massachusetts. He donated the remainder of his lands to the state in 1944, then leased back 107 acres around his mansion where he lived until his death in 1948 at the age of 84.

Essex

Phone Number
- (978) 887-5931

Website
- www.mass.gov/dcr/parks/northeast/brad.htm

Admission Fee
- None

Park Hours
- 8:00 a.m. to sunset, earlier for the state forest lands

Directions
- *Topsfield*; From Route 1 exit onto Ipswich Road and turn right on Asbury Street to the park entrance. For access to Willowdale State Forest, park on Ipswich Road.

The Walks

When teamed with the wilder Willowdale Forest next door there is just about any type of hike your dog desires at Bradley Palmer State Park. How about a pleasant streamside stroll? Check. Long rambles through uninterrupted woodlands? Check. A short hike around the landscaped grounds of a former estate? Check. Open fields and pasturelands not always found in Massachusetts parks? Check once more.

Your dog's hiking day will shuffle between unpaved roads, traditionally cut trails and bridle trails, especially if you cross Ipswich Road and test the going in the Willowdale State Forest.

Trail Sense: Trail maps are available in a kiosk outside the park headquarters so you can count on the box being filled.

Dog Friendliness

Dogs are welcome in the state park and state forest.

Traffic

Other trail users are much rarer in the less developed Willowdale State Forest. Don't be surprised to see an equestrian - Bradley Palmer's great passion - and hunting is allowed in November and December.

Canine Swimming

The Ipswich River is a suberb canine swimming hole; follow a fisherman's trail to get to an access spot.

Trail Time

Up to a full day is possible here.

The Arts and Crafts mansion house he called Willowdale was the pride and joy of Bradley Palmer's estate. Built in 1901, Palmer held lavish soirees here with distinguished guests such as General George Patton and the Prince of Wales.

33
Ward Reservation

The Park

Ward Reservation is the result of far-sighted preservationists who knitted together more than 40 separate parcels of farm and pasture land stretching for 17 miles. The properties cover 695 acres across all or portions of three hills - Shrub Hill, Boston Hill and Holt Hill.

The first gift of 153 acres came from Mrs. Charles Ward in 1940. The Ward property included Holt Hill, named for Nicholas Holt who first cleared land here in 1600s. At 420 feet, Holt Hill is the highest point in Essex County and Mrs . Ward assembled "Solstice Stones" on its summit where rocks are arranged in the shape of a compass. The largest stones were placed at the cardinal points and the north stone was marked.

The Walks

There are 13 miles of trails for your dog to test out in this sprawling park and long-distance canine hikers can summit all three hills. The closest to the car lot is the park star - Holt Hill, with clear views for your dog south to Boston. On June 17, 1775 townspeople climbed this hill to watch the burning of Charlestown by the British.

Your dog will meet a varied landscape of open fields and pastureland mixed with swamps and woodlands, especially if the *Ward Trail* is on your hiking itinerary. Moving beyond Holt Hill, this trail system is one of your best bets to disappear with your dog in the shadow of Boston.

Trail Sense: An accurate map can be printed from the website and may be available in the trailhead kiosk. The trails are somewhat marked and include at least one very useful sign: if you are making your way up the hill from the bog to the Solstice Stones there is a sign posted on a tree to the right of the trail just before crossing the road that tells you exactly how to do it.

Dog Friendliness

Dogs are welcome in Ward Reservation.

Traffic

This is a lightly visited park and if you venture beyond Holt Hill you are almost guaranteed to leave any trail users behind.

Canine Swimming

Hiking dogs only.

Trail Time

More than one hour.

The Solstice Stones laid out atop Holt Hill can serve several purposes: marking the time of year, viewing the Boston skyline or just relaxing.

34
Bash Bish Falls
State Park

The Park

Indian lore tells us of a young woman called Bash Bish, who lived in a village near these falls. Accused by a jealous friend of adultery she was sentenced to die. Bash Bish was strapped to a canoe and turned loose upstream from the deadly cataract. The canoe plunged into the falls and Bash Bish's body was never found.

When Bash Bish's young daughter, White Swan, grew up she often lingered sadly in the gorge and one day leapt to her death just before her lover Whirling Wind could reach her. She too was never found but it is said the images of Bash Bish and White Swan sometimes appear in the waters of Massachusetts' highest waterfall, almost 200 feet tall.

John Frederick Kensett, a leading member of the Hudson Valley School of artists, painted the falls in the 1850s. In 1860 the area was purchased by Jean Roemer, who built an elaborate Swiss-style chalet mansion that was to burn to the ground years later. The Massachausetts Department Environmental Management acquired 400 acres surrounding Bash Bish Falls in 1924.

Berkshire

Phone Number
- (413) 528-0330

Website
- www.mass.gov/dcr/parks/western/bash.htm

Admission Fee
- None

Park Hours
- Sunrise to sunset

Directions
- *Mt. Washington*; From Route 7 south of Great Barrington take Route 23/41 west for 4.9 miles to South Egremont. Turn left onto Route 41 South, then take the immediate right, Mount Washington Road, and continue as it becomes East Street. Turn right onto Cross Road then right onto West Street and continue for 1 mile. Turn left onto Falls Road and follow for 1.5 miles to the parking lot and trailhead on the left.

The Walks

Bish Bash Falls lies on the New York-Massachusetts border and can be reached from parking lots in either state. Adventurous dogs will want to pick their way down a serpentine trail from the Massachusetts side that will take

The final 80 feet of Bash Bish Falls are split by a diamond-shaped rock.

about twenty minutes. The New York route is longer - about one mile - but level the entire way. For extended time on the trail in the woods around Bash Bish that are peppered with hemlock trees. You can hook your dog up on the *South Taconic Trail* that passes around the park.

Trail Sense: There are mapboards and the trails are blazed. If you are unsure of your location, head for the roar of falling water.

Dog Friendliness
Dogs are welcome to visit Bash Bish Falls.
Traffic
Vehicles prohibited but expect plenty of folks joining you and your dog on the hike to the falls.
Canine Swimming
Not around these falls.
Trail Time
About an hour to hike to the falls and back.

35

Mount Everett
State Reservation

The Park

At 2,624 feet, Mount Everett is the dominant peak of the southwest Berkshire-Taconic range and the second tallest peak in Massachusetts. It is one of the oldest pieces of preserved land in the area. Along with Mount Greylock, Mount Everett was a piece of the first state park system in Massachusetts.

Mount Everett was named after Edward Everett, the famous 19th century Massachusetts orator best remembered for a speech no one remembers. In the ceremony to consecrate the national cemetery at Gettysburg in 1863 Everett delivered the main speech that streched for two hours and more than 13,000 words. After he sat down, Abraham Lincoln spoke for less than three minutes, delivering the immortal Gettysburg Address.

The Walks

There are two options for your dog to tag the summit of Mount Everett. From Guilder Pond the canine hike

Berkshire

Phone Number
- (413) 528-0330

Website
- www.mass.gov/dcr/parks/
western/meve.htm

Admission Fee
- None

Park Hours
- Sunrise to sunset

Directions
- *Mt. Washington*; From Route 7 south of Great Barrington take Route 23/41 West for 4.9 miles to South Egremont. Turn left onto Route 41 South, then take the immediate right, Mount Washington Road and continue as it becomes East Street. Turn left at the sign for Mount Everett and follow access road (open seasonally) past Guilder Pond to parking lot. To reach the Race Brook trailhead, continue on Route 41 South.

to the top is less than a mile - but 800 feet straight up - on a winding fire road. You'll join the *Appalachian Trail* (AT) for a narrow march to the summit on rocks that can be a challenge for your dog. If your dog doesn't mind the rocky going you can take the AT rather than the roomy dirt road. The *Guilder Pond Loop* works as a scenic leg-stretcher before your climb and the mountain lake is a perfect refresher for your dog after a spirited hike on Mount Everett.

The *Race Brook Trail* from Route 41 works past numerous water shoots and cascades before it reaches the AT in about two *tough* miles with the peak another mile to the north. Once on top you will be hiking through an unusal pitch pine-scrub oak ridgetop. Every now and then you will pop out onto a bare rock with the 360-degree views that visitors to Mount Everett have cherished for more than 100 years. The only thing remaining of the tower that once stood at the summit is a foundation, however.

Trail Sense: There are no maps on site so you will need to rely on blazes.

Dog Friendliness
Dogs are welcome to enjoy the Mount Everett views.
Traffic
Hikers only but expect plenty of company on splendid fall weekends.
Canine Swimming
Guilder Pond is an ideal canine swimming hole.
Trail Time
If your goal is just to reach the summit and get your dog back to your vehicle you can accomplish that in about an hour or you can hike with your dog all day.

Your dog will need bare spots on the rocks to see over the pitch pine and scrub oak atop Mount Everett into New York and Connecticut.

36
Windsor
State Forest

The Park

Windsor State Forest protects woodlands along the Westfield River that rushes energetically from the Berkshires to the Connecticut River. The upper Westfield River is one of the few successful spawning areas in the state for the Atlantic salmon.

Much of the river has been designated Wild and Scenic waters by the federal government. The watershed hosts the oldest continuously run white water canoe race in the United States, the Westfield River Whitewater Race, which is held every spring.

The park is most popular for its swimming area that sports a 100-foot sandy beach.

The Walks

The stand-out canine hike in the Windsor State Forest is the *Jambs Trail* to a narrow gorge where the Windsor Jambs Brook plunges through 80-foot high granite walls. Although less than one mile the trail, that begins behind the campground, picks its way deliberately along unfathomly green mosses and hemlocks to the Upper and Lower Jambs. The water spouts can only be viewed from above, with your dog safely behind a chain fence. You can use hard-packed dirt roads to complete a circuit back to the campground.

Berkshire

Phone Number
- (413) 684-0948

Website
- www.mass.gov/dcr/parks/western/wnds.htm

Admission Fee
- Parking fee in season

Park Hours
- Dawn to dusk; closes after Thanksgiving for the winter

Directions
- *Windsor*; The forest day-use area is on River Road between Route 9 and Route 116. From Route 8 in Dalton take Route 9 east for 11.3 miles to West Cummington. Turn left onto West Main Street; continue for .1 mile then take an immediate left onto River Road and follow for 2.9 miles to the day-use area entrance on the left. From the village of Savoy on Route 116 turn south onto River Road (unmarked). Follow River Road for 2.9 miles to the day-use area entrance on the right, or campground on the left.

Windsor offers more short hiking-only trails than the other state forests in the Berkshires. Three are available in the parking lot of the day use area, the sportiest being the *Steep Bank Brook Trail* that climbs back and forth across the tumbling stream. A hiking trail leads to the high point of 1,900 feet in the park; again use the network of dirt roads to close the loop.

Trail Sense: Park maps are available and the trails are blazed. The map is more reliable to unlock the maze of dirt roads than the road signs.

Dog Friendliness

Dogs are allowed on all Windsor trails but not allowed on the beach or in the swimming area in season.

Traffic

Most people come to Windsor for the swimming, not the trails. If you get tired of sharing the dirt roads with vehicles you can confine your explorations to the foot trails.

Canine Swimming

In the off-season your dog can enjoy the Westfield River.

Trail Time

Anywhere from an hour if you only want to see the Windsor Jambs or many hours using the other trails.

37
Noon Hill/ Shattuck Reservation

The Park

Noon Hill got its name because early settlers in Medfield knew it was mid-day when the sun cleared its 370-foot top. Or so the legend goes.

Later it came to be known as the place to quarantine towns folk suffering from smallpox during epidemics. Like everywhere else in Massachusetts Noon Hill was once cleared and farmed extensively. Holt Pond at the base of Noon Hill is man-made; it dates to 1764 and powered a saw mill.

The land was donated in 1959 by W.K. Gilmore & Sons Inc., purveyors in Wrentham of coal, grain, hay and cement since 1870. The adjoining Shattuck Reservation, 245 acres of Charles River floodplain, came from Henry Lee Shattuck, attorney and onetime member of the Massachusetts House of Representatives, in 1970.

Norfolk

Phone Number
- (781) 784-0567

Website
- www.thetrustees.org/ pages/342_noon_hill.cfm

Admission Fee
- None

Park Hours
- Sunrise to sunset

Directions
- *Medfield*; From the intersection of Routes 27 and 109 in Medfield, take Route 109 west for .1 mile and turn left immediately onto Causeway Street. Follow for 1.3 miles and turn left onto Noon Hill Road. A small parking area is .2 miles on the right.

The Walks

Your dog gets the choice of a trio of distinctly different trail experiences at these two connected reservations. The trek to the Noon Hill summit is not a problem for any level of canine hiker - the wide, woodsy path is generally flat save for the direct assault on the summit. Your dog's reward for this modest purchase is a southeast-facing overlook across the treetops.

The terrain flattens out completely in Shattuck Reservation, to its detriment when the Charles River spills over its banks. The connecting trail is narrow and twisting before reaching Causeway Street where several trail options reach to the meanders of the Charles River. The Reservation is a take-

out spot for float trips down the Charles and a great spot for your dog to slip in for a deep water swim.

The third option, more of a leg-stretcher than an adventure really, is a trip around Holt Pond. The trail is strewn with paw-friendly pine needles in many places and flat the whole way around.

Trail Sense: The reservation map is generally reliable but there are trail junctions that are not signed that can cause trouble (#8, please stand up). The trailheads on Causeway Street are not identified.

Dog Friendliness

Dogs can hike off-leash in the reservations; there is a two-dog limit on the trails, however. Dogs are not permitted in neighboring Medfield Rhododendrons Reservation.

Traffic

There is only room for a dozen or so cars in the lot; mountain bikes are restricted to certain trails that are not exciting to attract wheeled use.

Canine Swimming

Your dog can get a swim in Holt Pond but he will need to work a bit to get into the water. The dog paddling is splendid in the Charles River.

Trail Time

About two hours to fully explore both reservations.

38
Clarksburg State Forest

The Park

For the past 200 years Williams College students have had a tradition of hiking into the nearby mountains. A school holiday in the spring known as "Chip Day" was devoted to tagging nearby peaks. In the 1830s this study break would become known as "Mountain Day."

In 1915 the Williams Outing Club was formally organized, dedicated to blazing new trails around Williamstown, maintaining existing paths and promoting member outings. One of the club's most popular outing destinations is Pine Cobble, located in Clarksburg State Forest. Today the trail to the summit is maintained by a consortium of private owners, the Williams Outing Club and the Williamstown Rural Lands Foundation.

Berkshire

Phone Number
- None

Website
- www.wrlf.org/pinecobble.html

Admission Fee
- None

Park Hours
- Sunrise to one half-hour after-sunset

Directions (to *Pine Cobble Trail*)
- *Williamstown*; Take Route 2 east from its junction with Route 7. After .6 mile, turn left on Cole Avenue at the first stoplight. Cross the Hoosic River and make a right on North Hoosac Road. Follow for 1.8 miles and turn left on Pine Cobble Road to the parking area on the left, .2 of a mile up the hill. The trailhead is across the road.

The Walks

The canine hike to the Pine Cobble, long cherished for its expansive views from the top of 600-million year-old gray Cheshire quartzite cliffs, covers about two miles. You first tag the summit of East Mountain and then continue another half-mile to the 2,100 foot Pine Cobble. This is an energetic outing for your dog with a steady climb until the final few hundred yards where it becomes quite steep. If you choose to pause on the way up at this point, look around and enjoy a unique oak forest speckled with white pines. The route is rocky under paw but not as bad as some.

All dogs are happy to reach the open summit of Pine Cobble.

After your dog gets her fill of relaxing on the exposed cliffs with views on three sides you can penetrate into the lightly visited 3,000-acre state forest on the *Appalachian Trail.* There is about a four-mile stretch to the Vermont border - not that you're not allowed to leave the state and hike further with your dog.

Trail Sense: The way to the top is blazed liberally in light blue, with an occasional sign to help reinforce confidence.

Dog Friendliness
Dogs are welcome to make the climb to tag the Pine Cobble summit.
Traffic
Foot traffic only; the *Pine Cobble Trail* is within easy walking distance of the Williams College campus and gets plenty of use.
Canine Swimming
None.
Trail Time
About two hours; more if you take your dog down the *Appalachian Trail.*

39
F. Gilbert Hills State Forest

The Park

This is another recreation mecca the citizenry of Massachuestts has the Great Depression and the Civilian Conservation Corps (CCC) to thank for. But unlike its many brethren, the men of the 397-Veteran Corps Company, mostly military veterans from World War I, didn't spend much time building picnic areas and campgrounds. Instead they improved fire suppression, battled gypsy moth infestations and planted thousands of red pines. The camp in Foxboro State Forest, as it was known in the 1930s, lasted scarcely two years, not long compared to fellow CCC camps. The forest name today honors a Department of Conservation employee who produced a series of outstanding illustrative maps of many state owned properties.

Norfolk

Phone Number
- (508) 543-5850

Website
- www.mass.gov/dcr/parks/southeast/fgil.htm

Admission Fee
- None

Park Hours
- Sunrise to sunset

Directions
- *Foxboro*; From I-495 take Exit 14 onto Route 1 north. Turn right on Thurston Street that becomes West Street. Turn left on Mill Street to the forest headquarters and parking on the right.

The Walks

This state forest is the playground of serious canine hikers only. There are no swimming lakes here, no grassy fields for a game of fetch, no easy-strolling nature trails. The 23 miles of long looping trails are popular mostly with mountain bikers and in the drier months even host off-road vehicles. There are a few hiking-only trails but you won't be able to complete a loop without sharing the trail with the wheeled set.

For dogs who want to keep their adventures in F. Gilbert Hills to around an hour, set out on the *Blue Triangle Trail* behind park headquarters. The route trips through an agreeable mixed pine and oak woodland that is less rocky than most Massachusetts state parklands. For longer explorations the *Acorn*

Trail thrusts across the forest to the park landmark, High Rock. In the process it links up with the *Warner Trail*, marked by aluminum disks, that runs for 30 miles from Canton to Diamond Hill Park in Cumberland, Rhode Island. On May 19, 1951, Charlie Warner walked 25 miles on his trail when he was nearly 83 years of age. No word whether he had his dog with him.

Trail Sense: You can rely on the park map to tackle this extensive trail system with confidence.

Dog Friendliness

Dogs are welcome in the state forest.

Traffic

The trails will not be filled with casual hikers but if your dog doesn't enjoy mountain bikes and motorcycles this may not be fun.

Canine Swimming

An outing here will not include water time.

Trail Time

Many hours available.

40
Field
Farm

The Park

Parts of this property have been under cultivation since 1750. Two centuries later, after returning from service in World War II with the North Africa Tank Corps, Lawrence Bloedel purchased the former Nathan Field farm and abandoned his pre-war life as Williams College librarian.

In 1948 Lawrence and his wife Eleanore set about building a house to accommodate their expanding collection of contemporary American art. Frank Lloyd Wright was contacted for the commission but he demanded to design the furniture as well and Bloedel wanted to do that himself. Instead the couple retained Edwin Goodell who built a modern window-dominated home with simple lines. In 1966, Ulrich Franzen designed a Victorian Shingle-style house for the Bloedels' grandchildren, known as The Folly.

The Bloedels donated their blend of architecture and nature to the Trustees of Reservations in 1984 who manage the 316-acre property today.

Berkshire

Phone Number
- (413) 458-3135

Website
- www.thetrustees.org/pages/303_field_farm.cfm

Admission Fee
- None

Hours
- Sunrise to sundown

Directions
- *Williamstown*; At the intersection of Route 7 and Route 43, take Route 43 west and turn immediately onto Sloan Road on the right.

The Walks

The four-mile trail system at Field Farm is bisected by Sloan Road. All canine hiking here is easy-going with negligible elevation changes and mostly soft, paw-friendly paths. The star trails at Field Farm are the open field paths with views of the Taconic Range to the west and Mount Greylock to the east. Compared with the airy pastures and hayfields the oak and birch woodland trails are decidedly ordinary.

The *Oak Loop*, part of the stacked-loop trails on the north side of the property, is narrow and so non-descript you'll likely need your dog's nose to

Counterpoint, a welded steel masterpiece designed by Arline Shulman in 1971, sits in the garden at Field Farm with the Taconic Range as a backdrop.

follow it. The attached *Caves Trail* gains its distinction from a gaggle of small streams that disappear into a series of underground channels and limestone caves. The *South Trail*, across the road, pushes out through pastureland past the Field Farm's wetlands before looping on a small forest route.

Trail Sense: The trails are blazed but the park map is more reliable.

Dog Friendliness
Dogs can hike across these quiet trails.
Traffic
Foot traffic only.
Canine Swimming
A small pond is at the center of Field Farm.
Trail Time
More than one hour.

41

Joseph Allen Skinner State Park

The Park

Skinner State Park is home to Mount Holyoke, the westernmost peak on the Mount Holyoke Range. Its celebrated panoramic view of the valley below and highlands beyond made Mount Holyoke the second biggest tourist destination in America in the early 1800s, behind only Niagara Falls.

Recognizing the mountain's appeal, a group of businessmen from neighboring Northampton built the summit's first structure, a small cabin, in 1821. A hotel operated atop Mount Holyoke for 90 years beginning in the 1840s - an early tramway carried guests up the mountain. The enterprise was purchased by a group led by Joseph Allen Skinner in 1908, more one of preservation than profit as the automobile was opening newer horizons to vacationers. After a devastating hurricane crippled the hotel in 1938 Skinner gave the hotel, its related out buildings and 375 acres to the state. He asked for nothing in return, save that the park be named in his honor.

Hampshire

Phone Number
- (413) 586-0350

Website
- www.mass.gov/dcr/parks/
skinner/index.htm

Admission Fee
- None

Park Hours
- Sunrise to sunset

Directions
- *Hadley*; From I-91 southbound take Exit 19 to Route 9 east to Route 47 south; northbound take Exit 16 to Route 202 east and Route 116 north to Route 47 north.

The Walks

There are a dozen ways for your dog to scale the 940-foot summit of Mount Holyoke - probably more with a little imagination. Here are just four.

You can hike up the winding paved auto road, a popular activity when the 1.5-mile road is closed from mid-April to mid-November or on lightly visited weekdays. If your dog doesn't want to pound the pavement you can park at the Halfway House and take the hiking trail from this point, an historic route built by Amherst geology professor Edward Hitchcock in 1845. If your dog chides you for cheating you can take him to the top on any of several routes all the way from the bottom, beginning on Route 47.

For those with a car shuttle (or not) you can start at the Visitor Center on Route 116 and approach from 4.5 miles away on the *Metacomet-Monadnock Trail* (M-M). This will lead you across the Seven Sisters, a series of peaks that lead you up and down, but never jarringly.

The view of the Connecticut River valley from Mount Holyoke was one of the most famous in America in the 1800s.

Trail Sense: Mount Holyoke is well-mapped and marked.

Dog Friendliness
Dogs are welcome at Summit House, but not inside.
Traffic
Depending on your selected route you can encounter bikes, cars, horses.
Canine Swimming
None.
Trail Time
You will need at least two hours to reach the summit and return, regardless of what approach you take.

42
Mountain Meadow Preserve

The Park

Although less than 200 acres, Mountain Meadow Preserve packs plenty of diversity into your canine hike. Former farm fields have transitioned into wildflower meadows and grasslands - you can still spot abandoned farm machinery on the property.

The surrounding hills you visit next are spiked with pits and cleared roads, souvenirs from a mid-20th century gravel operation. With the tilling and digging over, Pamela Weatherbee, a local botanist and author of *Flora of Berkshire County*, donated the land to preserve the ecological diversity of Meadow Mountain.

The Walks

The canine hiking in the Preserve is divided into two loops, each an adventure unto itself. The first you reach with your dog is a circuit ringing an upland wildflower meadow. It is an easy ramble around the field but expect to stop plenty of times to admire the open views of the Taconic Range.

The second trail enters the hardwood forest to begin a jaw-shaped loop that will eventually find a ridgeline and top out at 1,120 feet. Your elevation gain will be 600 feet and staying straight on the trail will give you the less rigorous ascent.

Additional hiking with your dog is available by dropping onto a connector trail and climbing back around Mason Hill. Another connector leads into Vermont and the decaying homestead of Grace Greylock Niles, a 19th century naturalist noted for her popular book dealing with the swamp flora of the

Berkshire

Phone Number
- (413) 458-3144

Website
- www.thetrustees.org/pages/333_mountain_meadow_preserve.cfm

Admission Fee
- None

Hours
- Sunrise to sunset

Directions
- *Williamstown*; From the intersection of Routes 2 and 7 in Williamstown take Route 7 North. After crossing the Hoosic River start looking for Mason Street on the right. Turn onto Mason and continue to parking area at the end of the short residential street.

Hoosac valley, *Bog-Trotting for Orchids*. Look for foundation and wall ruins and cellar holes. All told, there are more than four miles of paw-friendly trails in the Mountain Meadow Preserve.

Trail Sense: There is a map posted at the trailhead and printed brochures are available. The mustard-colored blazes will take you confidently around.

Dog Friendliness

Dogs are permitted on the trails in the Preserve.

Traffic

Foot traffic only; the trails are also open for skiing. No hunting is allowed at Mountain Meadow.

Canine Swimming

None.

Trail Time

More than one hour.

These dogs are oblivious to the open views of the Taconic Range.

43
Mount Toby Demonstration Forest

The Park

Not much happened around Mount Toby, the dominant peak in the central Connecticut Valley, for more than 100 years from the time Captain Elnathan Toby, a settler from colonial Springfield became the first European to summit the mountain in the early 1700s. Unlike most hills in the state it was never logged, stone walls were never constructed for farms.

That changed in 1866 when the New London & Northern Railroad ran its first train along the east side of Mount Toby. In 1871, a lumberman named Rector Goss bought 206 acres

Franklin

Phone Number
- (413) 545-4358

Website
- nrc.umass.edu/index.php/facilities/our-forest-properties/mt-toby/

Admission Fee
- None

Park Hours
- Sunrise to sunset

Directions
- *Montague*; From the intersection of Routes 116 and 47 in Sunderland, follow Route 47 north to the town line with Montague. Just after the town line sign, turn right onto Reservation Road.
The gate, parking area and kiosk are 1/2 mile on the right. Access to Cranberry Pond is another 1/2 mile on the right.

of land here and built a railroad station near the base of the Roaring Brook Falls, a two-mile road to the top, and a six-story enclosed tower and stables on the summit. Goss died in 1875 and John L. Graves continued the dream of a mountain resort by building a hotel but just as it was finished in 1882 the tower, hotel and stables burned to the ground. The structures were never rebuilt and once again Mt. Toby lapsed into repose. In 1916, 755 acres became a demonstration forest for the University of Massachusetts.

The Walks

Two trails lead to the 1,269-foot summit: the old tower trail and a slice of the *Robert Frost Trail* that zigzags 47 miles up the eastern side of the Connecticut River. The latter is more of a pick-your-way hiking trail for your dog while the tower road is a delightful, winding route for much of its two miles in and out of thin and thick woods before beginning a rocky, steep ascent. Some of the larger trees in the forest will be encountered on the early steps of this journey.

Once on top you will need to scale the fire tower to get to the views above the treetops. Your dog can negotiate the wooden steps but must be leashed since the sides offer no protection on the way up. On a clear day the panorama can extend across the state and up the Connecticut River.

For further explorations a trail links the Mount Toby summit with Roaring Mountain (1,178 feet) although it is certainly a road less traveled. Roaring Brook Falls, located on the east side of the mountain, is a series of waterfalls, pools, potholes, chutes, and cascades that plummet one hundred feet over the rugged conglomerate ledges that comprise Mount Toby. The falls are most scenic in the spring and following periods of heavy precipitation; in the winter they are usually frozen over, and during dry periods the flow is often reduced to a trickle. Roaring Brook Falls is accessible by trail only.

Trail Sense: There is a mapboard to study at the parking lot before setting out but nothing to take along.

Dog Friendliness
Dogs are welcome to enjoy the climb to Mount Toby.
Traffic
This summit is one of the less frequented of the many mountains of the Connecticut Valley.
Canine Swimming
Cranberry Pond will serve nicely as a swimming hole for your dog after a spirited ascent of Mount Toby.
Trail Time
Allow two hours to reach the top, look around, and return.

44
Cape Cod Canal

The Park

It wasn't too long after the Pilgrims landed that dreamers began to look wistfully at the seven-mile isthmus of Cape Cod and envision a waterway that would eliminate the dangerous 165-mile ocean journey around the cape. But it wasn't until the early 1900s that the great ditch became a reality. August Belmont, best known for the New York subway and fast race horses, opened the Cape Cod Canal on July 29, 1914. But Belmont's canal wasn't wide enough or deep enough and enough mariners continued to ply the waters around the cape to make the canal a losing proposition.

Enter the federal government, which bought the canal in 1928. The waterway was dredged to 32 feet deep and widened to nearly 500 feet, the widest sea-level canal in the world. Ship traffic could safely transit the waterway and now over 20,000 vessels of all types use the Canal annually.

Barnstable

Phone Number
- (508) 833-9678

Website
- www.nae.usace.army.mil/recreati/ccc/ccchome.htm

Admission Fee
- None

Park Hours
- Sunrise to sunset

Directions
- *Buzzards Bay*; From the Sagamore Bridge take Exit 1C. Turn right onto Route 6A and drive under the Sagamore Bridge. After 1.3 miles turn left onto Tupper Road. Continue for .8 mile and turn left onto Freezer Road. Take the first right onto Ed Moffitt Drive and continue around the Coast Guard Station to the Vistitor Center at the end.

The Walks

When you hike with your dog around Massachusetts you will find there is usually one thing missing - the sun on the back of your dog's neck. There are a lot of trees in Massachusetts. And not many open-air parks. Sometimes you just want to get out and bask in the sunshine. The Cape Cod Canal is the place.

Service roads which parallel both sides of the Canal are available for bicycling, jogging and walking. Each service road is approximately seven miles long, with the distance between the Sagamore and Bourne Bridges a bit over three miles. The Canal provides a unique, close-up view of ocean-going ships to tugboats and everything in between.

For a dose of traditional hiking, the *Bournedale Hills Trail* extends 1.4 miles along the north side of the Canal from Bourne Scenic Park to Herring Run. The trail includes a .8-mile self-guided loop which interprets the Canal's historic and natural features. Within Scusset Beach State Reservation on the east end a short trail up Sagamore Hill provides access to the site of a World War II coastal fortification.

Trail Sense: The service roads are marked in half-mile increments so you can decide where to turn around. There are also historical interpretations on navigational poles along the way.

Dog Friendliness

Dogs are welcome to hike along the canal but are not permitted on the beach at Scusset Beach State Reservation.

Traffic

More than three million visitors come to the Cape Cod Canal each year so count on a communal dog-walking experience.

Canine Swimming

The swift currents suggest keeping your dog on shore on this one.

Trail Time

As long or as short as your dog desires.

45
Harvard Forest

The Park

For the first 300 years or so of this country Americans saw forests as soemthing to be cleared and utilized. If there was anything that was surely inexhaustible, it was trees. That began to change around 1900 when people began to look up and notice all the trees were gone from places and the concept of scientific forest management was born.

The Harvard Forest was one of the first. Founded by Richard Thornton Fisher in 1907, this 3000-acre woodland is one of the oldest and most intensively studied in North America. until his death in 1934.

Worcester

Phone Number
- (978) 724-3302

Website
- harvardforest.fas.harvard.edu/

Admission Fee
- None

Park Hours
- Sunrise to sunset

Directions
- *Petersham*; From Route 2 take Route 32 three miles south to the Fisher Museum on the left.

In the 1920s Fisher began sharing the university's findings with the public through a museum that became named for him. The core exhibit at the Museum consists of 23 three-dimensional dioramas portraying the history of central New England forests, their management, and ecology.

The Walks

There are two adjoining interpretive trails to explore with your dog in the Harvard Forest behind the Fisher Museum. The first leads around the John Sanderson farm that was first cultivated in 1764. Although only 500 yards long, the loop is stuffed with 27 learning stations so if you are hiking with an impatient dog you may want to proceed directly to the *Black Gum Trail*.

This 1.5-mile loop departs the pine plantations of the old Sanderson farm into a lovely hemlock forest. Look for trees with a strip of bark peeled off down the trunk. These were lucky survivors of a lightning strike in 1989 - trees struck by lightning typically shatter or catch fire.

If the weather has been wet, you won't need an interpretive sign to let you know when you enter the swamp. The flat, easy-walking trail will resemble the moist environs of its surroundings. Rare black gums, some as old as 300 years, grow here.

Trail Sense: Maps and descriptive flyers are available online and at the kiosk in front of the museum.

Dog Friendliness
Dogs are welcome in Harvard Forest.
Traffic
Horses and bikes are allowed but not usually found in abundance.
Canine Swimming
No opportunities here.
Trail Time
About one hour.

46
Minute Man
National Historic Park

The Park

Early on April 19, 1775, British soldiers marched from Lexington to Concord to tangle with 400 hastily assembled American militia. Afterwards the column of disciplined British regulars marched down the Battle Road back to Boston as Colinial militia sniped at them from behind barns and stone walls. By nightfall the British had suffered 73 deaths. Another 174 were wounded and many more missing. Forty-nine Americans were killed. Many of the sites in Concord, Lincoln and Lexington associated with the opening battle of the American Revolution, a battle that led to the creation of this country, were melded into the Historical Park in 1959.

Middlesex

Phone Number
- (978) 369-6993

Website
- www.nps.gov/mima/

Admission Fee
- None

Park Hours
- Sunrise to sunset

Directions
- *Concord*; From I-95 take Exit 30B onto Route 2A west. The park is 1-mile from the off-ramp.

The Walks

The heart of the park is the five-mile *Battle Road Trail* that is one of the most historic hikes you can take with your dog in America. Parking lots are spaced along the route so you can sample the Battle Road in chunks if your dog is not up to the entire trail. The ten-foot wide dirt-and gravel path is more paw-friendly than you would expect as it winds through wetlands and far more woodlands than the British would have seen when they marched through in 1775. Try to ignore the traffic noise from nearby Route 2A as you transport yourself back 235 years in history.

The two most famous sites on the trail are the Hartwell Tavern, an authentic period home, and the capture sit of Paul Revere. At the western terminus of the trail the house at Merriams Corner witnessed some of the toughest skirmishing on the first day of fighting in the American Revolution. The North Bridge is in a separate section of the park where your dog can stroll along a wide, shady path and up into open fields reminiscent of the terrain the day British and Americans faced off.

Trail Sense: Park maps are more necessary for driving directions than navigation by foot.

Dog Friendliness

Dogs are welcome outside the buildings in the Historical Park.

Traffic

Not too many visitors stray far from the major sites; expect to encounter cyclists on the *Battle Road Trail*.

While you enjoy the history of the North Bridge your dog will enjoy playing in the Concord River.

Canine Swimming

There is easy access to a doggie dip in the Concord River.

Trail Time

Several hours of trail time and more to study the wayside exhibits.

47
Stone Hill

The Park

Sterling Clark, an heir to the Singer sewing machine fortune, was an Army engineer decorated for his service in China supressing the Boxer Rebellion in 1905. Later, he returned to the remote expanses of northern China, leading a zoological expedition.

He began collecting art in 1912 and amassed a formidable private collection with his wife Francine, a former French actress. In 1950 the couple purchased property in Williamstown to house their art. The museum opened in 1955, bringing the impressive collection to the public for the first time. To celebrate its 30th anniversary the trails were cut around the 140-acre grounds in 1985.

Berkshire

Phone Number
- None

Website
- None

Admission Fee
- None

Park Hours
- Sunrise to sunset

Directions
- *Williamstown*; At the intersection of Routes 7 and 2 in town proceed all the way around a small rotary past the Williams Inn and the public library. Turn right onto South Street and proceed to the Clark Art Institute on the right. Go through the underpass and park at the back of the visitor lot behind the museum.

The Walks

The foot paths around the Clark Institute offer a pleasing mix of forest and open fields for your dog to enjoy. Heading up from the parking lot the route climbs steadily - but not arduously - until you reach the wide Stone Hill road that was once the main north-south passage through Berkshire County before Route 7 came to pass. The trail reaches its apex at an intersection marked by a carved stone seat.

Your return to the right brings your dog down through a hillside pasture with panoramic views of the town and mountains as you descend. This is some of the best open-field canine hiking in the Berkshires. You can slice your 1.5-mile excursion in half by just taking this *Pasture Loop*.

At the trailhead are two small gravestones for the dogs that belonged to the one-time owner of the property, Dr. Vanderpool Adriance.

This stone seat was a tribute from the town to a Williams College professor wrongly thought to be a German spy during World War I.

Trail Sense: There is no trail map but the paths are well-blazed. You will notice additional unmarked routes here and there so feel free to go off the grid and explore.

Dog Friendliness
Dogs are welcome on the Clark Institute grounds.
Traffic
Stone Hill is a popular walking destination for town residents.
Canine Swimming
This is a completely dry canine hike.
Trail Time
About one hour.

48
Myles Standish State Forest

The Park

Much of the land south of Plymouth Center is comprised of a unique pitch pine/scrub oak eco-system known as "pine barrens." To the early settlers this land was useless, a place to hunt and cut down fire-wood but you couldn't farm here. In 1709, 30,000 acres of this unprofitable scrub was divided into ten "great lots" and divvied up among 200 heirs of the original "purchasers" who assumed the colony debt in 1628.

Fast forward a couple of hundred years. By 1913, it is estimated that Massachusetts has 1,000,000 acres of dangerous "waste land" that is littered by the tops of felled trees and ignitable tinder. The state began purchasing large swaths of such land and in 1916 Massachusetts had its first state forest, named for the military commander of Plymouth Colony.

Plymouth

Phone Number
- (508) 866-2526

Website
- www.mass.gov/dcr/parks/southeast/mssf.htm

Admission Fee
- None

Park Hours
- Sunrise to sunset

Directions
- *South Carver*; Take I-495 to Exit 2 and go north on Route 58. Turn on Cranberry Road and follow into the forest.

The Walks

Myles Standish State Forest is the largest publicly owned recreation area in southeastern Massachusetts and brings with it some big numbers: 570 camp-sites, 35 miles of equestrian trails and 13 miles of hiking trails, 16 ponds...

Clearly a busy place, best visited in slack times when the paved multi-use trails quiet down. The foremost hiker-only trail can be found behind the park office on the *East Head Reservoir Nature Trail*. The reservoir is the larg-est body of water in the park, built in 1868. This is one of the supreme lake circumnavigations in the state with the water (stored to flood cranberry bogs, not to drink) in sight most of the way around, save for when you are tunneling through thick high bush blueberries. The surface is paw-friendly sandy loam and pine straw and there are just enough places to swim to keep your dog happy without being so many that you never finish the 3.1-mile loop. Like most of the forest trails, this is flat, easy going.

Trail Sense: Although large, this is is not a complex trail system. The trails have enough plastic trinagle markers and the map is reliable.

Dog Friendliness
Dogs are allowed on the trails and in the campground.
Traffic
If you hike along the paved bike paths and roads expect any manner of wheeled conveyance; the hiking-only trails will provide a bit of solitude, even on a summer weekend.
Canine Swimming
Dogs are not allowed on the beaches in-season and the shoreline of some of the kettle ponds in protected.
Trail Time
More than one hour.

49
Mount Pisgah
Conservation Area

The Park

The Mt. Pisgah complex of lands comprises some 5,000 acres in parts of Boylson, Berlin, Bolton, and Northborough. Still wild and rural, much is still managed woodland and farmland. Since the roads carry little traffic and hence lessen their barrier effect for wildlife, animals have been observed here that are not usually seen in this part of the state, including bobcat, black bear, and moose.

Mount Pisgah, at 715 feet, is the highest point in Northborough. The Conservation Area is cobbled together from four adjacent tracts of land.

The Walks

This is one of the best places in Massachusetts for beginning canine hikers. The trails are well-blazed and well-maintained and sweeping views can be achieved with very little purchase. The *Mentzer Trail* that leads from the trailhead to the North Overlook with little elevation gain is the prettiest, paw-friendliest trail at Mount Pisgah. It also features some of the largest trees and crosses the pleasing Howard Brook. You can warm your dog up with a short jaunt around the moist, richly vegetated *Loop Trail*.

Once your dog gets her legs under her you can set out for more challenging fare on the more than five miles of trail that course through the four adjacent tracts. A wide, old cart road, the Berlin Road Trail, connects the trail systems in the southern and northern regions of the park. The trails get a bit steeper and rootier under paw. The summit offers no views and, unless your dog needs to

Middlesex

Phone Number
- (978) 443-5588

Website
- www.sudburyvalleytrustees.org/maps?q=node/164

Admission Fee
- None

Park Hours
- Sunrise to sunset

Directions
- *Berlin*; From I-495 take Exit 26 to Route 62 west, towards Berlin/Clinton. Pass through the center of Berlin and bear left onto Linden Street at the flashing yellow light. Follow Linden Street for 1.6 miles and turn left onto Ball Hill Road. Follow the road, which becomes Smith Road, for 1.3 miles. A small parking lot will be on the left.

check it off her life-list of tagging Massachusetts mountains, you can bypass it altogether on the *Tyler Trail*.

Trail Sense: Print a trail map online to be on the safe side. The trails are energetically marked.

Dog Friendliness

Dogs are welcome to go off-leash but must be tethered when approaching other trail users. There is a three-dog maximum at Mount Pisgah.

Traffic

You are unlikely to have to shoehorn your dog into any crowds at the overlooks here; mountain bikes are allowed.

Canine Swimming

Howard Brook can provide a lively splash but no more.

Trail Time

You can keep it under an hour or spend several hours in the Mount Pisgah woods.

The only view on the Mount Pisgah summit is of this artistic cairn.

50
October Mountain State Forest

The Park

October Mountain - the name may have come from Herman Melville - is the Goliath of Massachusetts state forests at 16,500 acres. The impetus for its formation came in 1915 when a group of Berkshire men pledged $25,000.00 to enable the Commonwealth to buy the 11,000 acre William C. Whitney estate for $60,000. The Schermerhorn family, of Lenox and New York, then donated the 1,000-acre scenic Schermerhorn Gorge to the project. The state forest opened to the public that same year.

Whitney served as Secretary of the Navy under Grover Cleveland and used some 1000 acres of his private wilderness as a hunting range where buffalo, elk, Virginia deer, angora sheep and moose grazed. Frederic Law Olmsted's firm designed the landscaping and cowboys led hunting parties. After Whitney's wife died, he sold the animals to zoos and abandoned the estate.

During the Great Depression of the 1930s, Franklin Roosevelt's "Tree Army," the Civilian Conservation Corps, planted over 960 acres in conifers. Today there is hardly any place for a buffalo to turn around for all the trees, let alone roam.

Berkshire

Phone Number
- (413) 243-1778

Website
- www.mass.gov/dcr/parks/western/octm.htm

Admission Fee
- None

Hours
- Sunrise to one-half hour after sunset

Directions
- *Lee*; From Exit 2 of the Massachusetts Turnpike go 1 mile on US 20 West. Turn left onto Maple Street and bear right at upcoming intersections to Woodland Road, that reaches to the campground.

The Walks

October Mountain is not the place to come for a casual canine hike. Without a four-wheel drive vehicle you won't be able to penetrate much more than the perimeter of the forest. The primary foot trail here is the *Appalachian Trail* that rambles over Becket (2,200 feet) and Walling (2,220 feet) mountains in its 10-mile course through the park. You can sample this trail with your dog by taking Becket Road off of Route 20. After Becket becomes Tyne Road pull to the left on a dirt road and park. Hike on a gradual ascent on this road for less than two miles where it joins the *Appalachian Trail* and then drops down to the shore of Finerty Pond. You can return south on the *Cordonier Trail* and use Becket Road to close a six-mile loop.

If you are staying in the campground, a good option is to head north on the *Eagle Ledge Trail* to explore the Schermerhorn Gorge on the *Gorge Trail* as it heads into Felton Lake. You can also park at Woods Pond for this canine hike.

Trail Sense: A trail map is available - and a must.

Dog Friendliness
Dogs are permitted to hike in the state forest and campground.
Traffic
Save for the Appalachian Trail, most forest trails are multi-use; ATVers can ride down designated trails.
Canine Swimming
The ponds in October Mountain are a prime attraction for canine hikers.
Trail Time
A full day and more are possible.

51
Elm Bank Reservation

Norfolk County

Wellesley;one mile west of town on Washington Street (Route 16).

This was the 198-acre estate of Benjamin Pierce Cheney, a former stagecoach driver whose express line between Boston and Montreal became the foundation for American Express. In 1874 he used some his $10,000,000 fortune to buy the manor house on the Charles River. He spent his final 20 years installing gardens and conservatories on the grounds. He also helped found the Massachusetts Horticultural Society.

When he died, the property passed to his daughter, who replaced his wood Victorian house with a 43-room Georgian-style brick mansion designed by Alexander Jackson Davis, the architect behind the New York Public Library. After Alice Cheney-Baltzell's death the property passed to the Stigmatine order of monks, who used the manor as a boys' school; when they closed its doors the house stood vacant for two decades until the Horticultural Society took it over from the state on a $1-a-year-for-99-years lease.

Your dog will have plenty of canine company on an outing at the old Cheney place. The hiking takes place on a finger of land surrounded on three sides by the Charles River as it folds back on itself. The woodland (pines on the western edge, hardwoods in the eastern bottomlands) is covered by a wide, paw-friendly natural loop. It is so agreeable your dog just may demand a second go-round - and you may do so involuntarily as the paths are not marked. Not to worry; you can never go too far astray. There are two excellent spots for your dog to jump into the Charles, one on the west side and one near the point to the north.

52
World's End Reservation

Plymouth County

Hingham; end of Martin's Lane. From Route 3, take Route 228 North (Exit 14) for 6.5 miles. Turn left on Route 3A and follow for .4 mile. Turn right onto Summer Street and at the traffic light with Rockland Street and on to Martins Lane.

Over the years this peninsula has been considered for one of America's pioneering residential subdivisions, as the site for the United Nations headquarters and a nuclear power plant. But despite the threats from this intimidating trio and others nothing was ever built at World's End. Boston businessman John Brewer was the wealthy owner who created a waterside estate here in the 1800s.

In 1890 he hired Frederick Law Olmsted to design that housing development and Olmsted built serpentine carriage paths and planted trees. But the project stalled so all that remains are the paths, the trees and swaying grasses.

The carriageways can be a bit rocky under paw but your dog will likely forgive you as she trots around this delightful park. World's End is comprised of four drumlins, glacial hills, that top out at 120 feet. The trail system piles loops around and across the hilltops with about four miles of carriageways. There are some detours to explore as well, through a salt marsh and out to rocky shorelines. On top of the open hilltops you will see downtown Boston about 15 miles away across the harbor. Your dog can get in the water for a swim and the stone water fountain features run-off into a dog-high drinking bowl.

53
Nantucket Island
Barnstable County
Nantucket; on Madaket Road west of Main Street.

Beginning with an initial donation of less than one acre in 1963, the Nantucket Conservation Foundation is now the Island's largest landowner, with 8,700 acres - 29% of the Island's total land area. Dogs are allowed on most of the properties, dogs are allowed on most of the beaches year-round and dogs are even allowed on the shuttle buses to the beach. Too bad this tail-wagging paradise is 30 miles off-shore.

If you only have one hike to take with your dog on the Island, make it at Sanford Farm. The romp across Anne Sanford's old estate on smooth, roomy dirt-and-grass paths will be about as much fun as your dog can have in Massachusetts. The full loop of the 600+ acres will cover an easy six miles (the high point on the trail at Pasture Overlook tops out at about 49 feet) but alternate loops can break off your adventure before that. There are kettleponds, pine plantations, windswept pastures, Trots Swamp, the Atlantic Ocean - and interpretive markers all along the way so you don't miss a thing.

54
Middlesex Fells Reservation
Middlesex County
Stoneham and other towns; on Route 28 off either Exit 33 or 35 of I-93.

In 1890 landscape architect Charles Eliot got an open letter published in a New England periodical called *Garden and Forest*. Eliot proposed the immediate preservation of "special bits of scenery" still remaining "within ten miles (16 km) of the State House which possess uncommon beauty and more than usual refreshing power." Eliot went on to urge that legislation be enacted to create a nonprofit corporation to hold land for the public. The next year the Massachusetts Legislature did exactly that, establishing The Trustees of Public Reservations "for the purposes of acquiring, holding, maintaining and opening to the public beautiful and historic places within the Commonwealth."

Virginia Wood, donated by the Tudor family in the name of their daughter who was killed in a riding accident, was the first tract of Massachusetts land acquired by the Trustees. Development would become a hallmark of the park over the years, a process that would challenge the ideal of "uncommon beauty." By 1897 the park was over 3,000 acres including 1,200 acres of water bodies, 13 miles of wood roads, eight miles of town roads, farms, private estates and the Langwood Hotel. There was a zoo in the early 1900s and an electric trolley arrived in 1910. In the 1920s a half million trees were planted. A swimming pool followed and a skating rink. And a soap box derby track. The most lasting impact would occur in the 1960s when the interstate highway system cleaved the park in two.

If you are looking for your dog to run in a pack, Middlesex Falls is your place. The Sheepfold, an open pasture where flocks of sheep grazed into the 1900s, is always a whirl of wagging tails where city folk bring their dogs. There are plenty of trails to head down with your dog but if you are out for a serious hike, parting with a few bucks for a trail map is a wise investment. There is no mapboard on site and the maze of pathways is indecipherable without local knowledge. The orange-blazed *Reservoir Trail* visits three ponds in an easy five miles; more experienced canine hikers will favor the *Skyline Trail*. "Fells" is the Saxon word for rocky, hilly tracts of land and your dog's paws will undoubtedly agree. Parking can be problematic around Middlesex Fells and the Sheepfold lot doesn't open until 9:00 a.m.

55
Monroe State Forest

Franklin County

Monroe; on Zoar/River Road, 11 miles north of Route 2, 2.2 miles west of Charlemont center.

There is some debate over whether the Eastern Hemlock and hardwood forests in Monroe are true old-growth or only second-growth; don't let your dog get caught up in the semantic game - there are some very large trees here. The Henry David Thoreau Pine, located along Dunbar Brook, is considered to be New England's only known member of the elite 12 x 160 club, that is a girth more than 12 feet and a height over 160 feet.

You can take your dog on an easy, satsifying exploration of that Dunbar Brook as it hurries over mossy boulders during a race down 700 feet of mountain valley in two miles. You can also fill up your dog's hiking day in Monroe State Forest; a one-way hike to the Raycroft Lookout, built by the Civilian Conservation Corps in the 1930s, covers three miles and a loop of the park will cover about nine miles, taking in the 2,730-foot summit of Spruce Mountain.

The town of Monroe is the second smallest in the Commonwealth. Even if all 93 citizens showed up here at once, the trails still would not be crowded.

56
Mohawk Trail State Forest

Franklin County

Charlemont; on Route 2, four miles west of town center.

Only a state park in Pennsylvania has more 150-foot trees than the Mohawk Trail State Forest. Numerous individual trees of a dozen species have been confirmed to surpass 200 years of age but the lord of the forest is the white pine. The tallest single tree in New England, the Jake Swamp Pine (named after a Mohawk Indian tribal chief) has been accurately measured at 168.5 feet high.

The *Mahican-Mohawk Trail* to the lower meadows passes through some of the tallest of the pines. This route is part of the historic Native American foot path that connected the Connecticut and Hudson River valleys. The state forest was established in 1921, a few years after the Mohawk Trail (Route 2) was paved to speed travelers from Boston to New York.

South of Route 2, the *Totem Trail* climbs moderately for a bit over a mile to a rock outcropping overlooking the Deerfield River, a popular whitewater destination. This is an out-and-back affair for your dog.

57
Norris Reservation
Plymouth County

Norwell; from Route 3 take Exit 13 onto Route 53 North. Turn right onto Route 123 for three miles to Norwell Center. Upon entering the town veer right onto West Street that ends quickly on Dover Street. The park entrance is to the left across the road.

The beauty of the woodlands and flowering azaleas belie this site's industrial past. In 1690, Second Herring Brook was tapped to run a gristmill, and later a sawmill. Along the North River that forms the back boundary of the 129-acre reservation shipyards thrived for 200 years, launching tall-masted wooden ships on the tides. Until the shipwrights left after the Civil War more than 1,000 boats were built on the North River.

In the 1920s Albert and Eleanor Norris began purchasing land along the North River. They built a cottage and cut a system of wide trails that is used today. This is two miles of easy going for your dog on the series of stacked loops - you can choose how much or how little you want to enjoy these tame woodlands.

Along the way are remants of the bustling industry that once defined the North River - a dam for the millpond, stone walls from the days of grazing cattle and an empty boathouse for watching the tidal river flow. Although problematic, a determined dog can get into the river for a swim.

58
Ellisville Harbor State Park
Plymouth County

Plymouth; on Route 3A, two miles north of Route 3, Exit 2.

You can't hike with your dog anywhere in Massachusetts like Ellisville Harbor. The wide gravelly trail in this former 18th century farmstead begins on a bluff above a salt marsh and winds through a red pine forest down to the shoreline some 15 minutes later. Dogs are restricted from beachcombing during nesting time for the piping plover but can always get at least a swim in Cape Cod Bay in front of the wooden steps.

Along the way a short detour leads down to the edge of the salt marsh and you can go off-trail with your dog into the rolling meadows that have been maintained as grasslands and frequently have wide mown swaths for walking.

59

Wachusett Mountain State Reservation
Worcester County
Princeton; on Mountain Road off Mile Hill Road from Route 140, two miles south of Route 2, Exit 25.

Retreating glaciers left Wachusett Moutnain standing alone, a monadnock - from the Algonquin word for "a mountain that stands alone." At 2,006 feet Wachusett is the highest mountain in Massachusetts east of the Connecticut River. With a large, flat summit there are 360-degree views that include the Boston skyline to the east.

A hotel appeared on the summit in 1882; the first of 22 ski trails, *Pine Hill Trail*, was cut in 1934. The longest T-bar in New England was constructed at Wachusett Mountain in 1962 (3,800 feet). The hotel was destroyed by fire in 1970 but that has hardly dulled interest in the mountaintop - 600,000 people come each year.

Almost all the canine hiking here involves going to the top on Wachu-sett Mountain one way or another. The most direct route is up that *Pine Hill Trail*, a steep, rocky ascent that is aided by stone steps cut into the trail. The recommended route from the Visitor Center is as follows: start south on the *Bicentennial Trail* and take the second right onto the *Loop Trail*. Follow *Loop* until it meets *Mountain House Trail* and take a right. Continue on *Mountain House* to the Summit. Coming down take the *Pine Hill Trail* (to the left of the road) down to *Bicentennial Trail* and retrace your steps to the left back to the Visitor Center to complete the 1.5-mile journey.

You can also park on your way up the auto road beneath the summit and jump onto one of the footpaths leading to the top. Long-distance options highlight some of the park's natural wonders. Approaching from the north you pass Balance Rock, two large boulders that glaciers stacked one atop the other. Coming from the south, the *Harrington Trail* passes through a rare old growth forest of red oaks and hemlocks where some of the giants were standing before the American Revolution.

60
Jacobs Hill

Worcester County

Royalston; on Route 68 a half-mile north of town.

The land for this park was acquired in 1975 with funds provided anonymously, which is appropriate since hiking with your dog here has the feel of discovering something little known. A balloon trail covers about two miles and takes in three memorable destinations: two overlooks of the Tully River from exposed ledges at either end of the reservation and Spirit Falls that lives up to its name as it charges off the ridgeline. The water is fed from a black spruce and tamarack bog known as Little Pond.

The terrain under paw is almost always interesting whether pine straw or mossy rocks as it rolls up and down. Jacobs Hill is part of the 22-mile *Tully Trail* that loops through largely undeveloped Tully Valley. If your dog wants extra trail time here but doesn't want to spend the entire day on the *Tully Trail* it is possible to loop around the Tully River on the eastern side of the loop, through Tully Campground. The trails are well-marked and signed at critical junctions. If you do attempt the complete *Tully Trail* be aware that you will be leading your dog down two-lane backroads at times.

Your trail dog will look forward to the doggie spa that is Spirit Falls.

61
Shaker Mountain

Berkshire County

Hancock; on Route 20, 5.5 miles west of Route 7.

The Shakers, so named for their frenzied religious dancing, trace their beginnings to Manchester, England, in 1747. As Millennialists, they believed that Christ's second coming was realized in their leader, Mother Ann. Misunderstood and persecuted, Mot-her Ann Lee sailed to America in 1774 with eight Shaker converts to lead a life of simplicity and pacifism. She came to preach to farm families in this area in 1783 and in 1790 Hancock Shaker Village was established.

The Shaker population reached its peak in the mid-19th century, with an estimated 4,000 to 5,000 Shakers. Shaker communities were required to clear the summit of a nearby hill for worship. The site chosen was atop Mt. Sinai, now known as Shaker Mountain, around 1842.

By the 1960s the sites of Shaker rituals had been long forgotten when John Manners, a local hiker, stumbled across some overgrown foundations. Over the next 25 years Manners and the Boy Scouts of America cleared trails and identified historic remains.

The exploration of Shaker Mountain and its fellow peak, Holy Mount, takes place in the southern end of Pittsfield State Forest. The Hancock Shaker Trail covers about six miles and is rich in religious and industrial significance. Along the way you'll take your dog past house and mill foundations, dams and marvelous remains of stone walls.

The trail first winds to the top of 1,845-foot Mt. Sinai (Shaker Mountain) using a combination of narrow footpaths and rocky cart roads. You can cut your canine hiking day in half by heading back after descending through a hemlock forest at this point or continue on to loop over Holy Mount. The cart roads here can fill with water when wet and stream crossings aren't always bridged.

The trail leads to two Shaker sacred sites that have been levelled out on the top of Mt. Sinai and Holy Mount. When the Shakers worshipped here non-believers were not allowed on these grounds. A reservoir is ideally situated for a refreshing doggie dip at the end of this adventure.

62
Four Ponds Conservation Area

Barnstable County
North Pocasset; on Barlows Landing Road east of County Road; west of Route 28.

The four namesake ponds are not accidental - in 1776 a miller named Jesse Barlow dammed a stream and built a gristmill on the Pocasset River. In the 1820s additional ponds were built so the Pocasset Iron Foundry could process the area's bog ore.

The canine hiking is easy-going on dirt roads and walking paths through a delightfully mixed forest. The trails liberally visit the sandy-bottomed ponds, sometimes crossing atop the dikes that birthed them. Small bridges carry your dog across Trout Brook. Bikes are allowed but only on a few trails in the back of the park that joins the Bourne Town Forest and bumps the available trail time to over an hour. Although the park is hardly hidden, being not far from the millions of cars using Route 28 each year, don't be surprised if you are alone with your dog here.

63
Granville State Forest

Hampden County
Granville; on unimproved West Hartland Road 1.6 miles south of Route 57, 23 miles west of Exit 3 off I-91.

The Hubbard River is the star of this remote 2,426-acre forest on the Connecticut border. In 1749, the first English pioneer to this region, Samuel Hubbard, homesteaded along its banks. A walking path traces the river for more than two miles as it squeezes through natural rock formations. There are more rocks than water in most places so the river is usually better for splashing than swimming for your dog.

If starting in the campground the trail along Halfway Brook - no slouch in the scenery game itself - leads to the Hubbard River. That campground only has 22 sites so the 17 miles of forest trails are almost always empty. Most trails travel long distances from the limited parking areas so this is not a destination for casual canine hikers. Across West Hartland Road the trails flatten out considerably.

64
Lynn Woods

Essex County

Lynn; on Pennybrook Road off Walnut Street, two miles east of the Saugus exit off Route 1.

In 1658, a pirate ship anchored in Lynn Harbor and the privateers came ashore seeking to exchange silver for tools from the Saugus Iron Works. British soldiers intervened, capturing and hanging the crew, save for a Thomas Veal who escaped into what is now Lynn Woods, presumably with a fortune in booty in tow. Without a ship, Veal integrated into the community, living in a natural cave until an earthquake shook loose a gigantic rock that permanently sealed the cave opening, trapping the buccaneer and his treasure forever in Dungeon Rock.

Fast forward 200 years. Hiram Marble, a Spiritualist who believed in communication with the deceased, got a message from the ghost of Thomas Veal who told him to dig at Dungeon Rock to become rich. So dig he did. And blast. And chisel. After ten years Marble's tunnel at Dungeon Rock was over 130 feet long - it didn't go in a straight line, there were numerous turns where he was guided by voices from the other side. Still he dug, finally dying in 1868 at the age of 65. Edwin Marble succeeded his father in this quixotic quest. He became ill from digging in the damp, dark cavern and on January 16, 1880, at the age of 48, he too died. He was buried near the foot of the rock, as this was his desire.

In the end the Marbles did not dig to become rich; they toiled day after day to prove they could communicate with people in the afterlife. After decades of living in the beautiful woods the Marbles planned to take the treasure and purchase as much land as possible for the people of Lynn to enjoy forever. It could be said the citizens of Lynn got the treasure when the Lynn Woods Reservation was founded in 1881 the year after Edwin Marble died. With 2,200 acres it is the second largest municipal park in Greater Boston.

There are 30 miles of trails here, enough so that many are devoted to foot traffic only. The most popular routes lead to the 200-foot hills south of Walden Pond, including Burrell Hill upon which sits the 48-foot Stone Tower, constructed during the Depression. Lynn Woods excels for hiking destinations with swamps, glacial erratics, Boston views and cliffs. A detailed grid-style map is critical to finding them all - hopefully one will be available at the park gate. The Dungeon Rock tunnel is usually open for exploration (bring a flashlight) Tuesday through Saturday.

65
Beebe Woods Conservation Area

Barnstable County

Falmouth; west of town on Highfield Drive off Depot Avenue from North Main Street off Route 28

When asked why he robbed banks, career bank robber Willie Sutton answered, "Because that's where the money is." Sometimes when you are looking for a place to hike with your dog it is easiest to just go where the dogs are. Around Falmouth, that would be Beebe Woods.

This land was held in common for the first settlers and they dutifully cleared away every stick for lumber, firewood and fence posts. Once the trees were harvested the cleared land became pasture for sheep and cattle. James Madison Beebe bought his property land here in 1872 and eventually accumulated 708 acres. The land stayed in the family for 60 years; summer homes were built and carriage paths graded. Development gnawed away the parcel until 1976 when Josiah Lilly III conveyed 383 acres to the Town of Falmouth for conservation.

Miles of shaded carriage and single track trails, access to two ponds and the interestingly variable terrain all conspire to lure dog walkers to Beebe Woods. Most of the trail users will have an off-leash dog or two. The park has many looping, intersecting trails but the best canine hike will find a way to the deep, clear waters of Deep Punch Bowl Pond.

66
John Drummond Kennedy Park

Berkshire County

Lenox; on Route 7A, just south of the intersection with Route 7/20, parking is available at the Lenox House or atop the hill at the Church on the Hill.

On this property at 1,460 feet above sea level in 1902 General Thomas Hubbard built the resplendent Aspinwall Hotel. The colonnaded, Spanish-style hostelry hosted high society in 400 elegant rooms - each with its own fireplace. The Aspinwall even boasted a resident orchestra so guests could enjoy music as they lounged on the veranda enjoying views of the Catskills and the Green Mountains. The resort flourished until a fire burned it to the ground in 1931. The Aspinwall was never rebuilt and the property sat idle until the town of Lenox purchased 450 acres here in 1957.

Your dog will take immediately to these wide, well-groomed trails - 31 in all. If you have trouble making up your mind, head out on the #1 (*Main Trail*), that dissects the park for its entire length, or the #11 (*Overlook Trail*) from the West Dugway entrance. As you wander along you can check out the landscape and decide on how to spend the remainder of your canine hiking day in Kennedy Park.

There is plenty to set your dog to panting here as you are almost always moving up or down through these attractive woods. Unlike many parks with reforested farmlands in much of the Berkshires, you will find some of the county's largest trees here.

67
Old Town Hill

Essex County

Newbury; from I-95 take Exit 54 and follow Route 133 East to Route 1. Turn left and follow 4.8 miles to Boston Road. Turn right and bear right on Hay Road in .3 miles. After one mile turn right on Newman Road to parking lot on left.

When Newbury was young, 168-foot Old Town Hill was the "Great Hill." The townsfolk built their first Meeting House on the Lower Green at the foot of the hill in 1634. On top of the hill thousands of cattle and sheep grazed and the scalped crest was clear enough for a sentry box to be installed. Today's hill, with every inch covered in forest, would not be recognized by those residents as their "old town hill." What they might recognize are the tidal salt marshes along the Parker River where salt hay was harvested with horse-drawn mowing machines.

The canine hiking at Old Town Hill takes place on opposite sides of Newman Road, each holding a vastly different experience for your dog. On the parking lot side the *River Trail* slinks down to Little River and back. The bank is a couple feet above the water but an athletic dog can access the water - be careful, however, the current is fast.

Across the road you can hop on the *Bay Circuit Trail* for a loop to views that peek out from the trees atop Old Town Hill. Use the *North Loop Trail* to close your circle; there are additional trails to be had but, like the *Bay Circuit* they will land you on the two-lane road that has no shoulders.

68
Chester-Blandford State Forest

Hampden County

Chester; on Route 20 between exits 2 and 3 of the Massachusetts Turnpike.

The shiny flakes your dog is likely to see under his paws here are flecks of mica and quartz, often indicators of gold. Prospectors have indeed pulled nuggets from Gold Mine Brook but nothing to make anyone rich. Small mines did operate here but produced mica, emery and corundum.

There are two points of destination in Chester-Blandford State Forest, each radiating in a different direction from the parking lot. Straight ahead on the gravelly but wide Sanderson Brook Road is a well-marked turn-off (look for an acorn blaze) for Sanderson Brook Falls. The waters course over a 60-foot face of a rock wall before erupting into cascades below. The trail leads to the base of the falls where the plunge pool is too shallow for serious dog paddling but refreshing nonetheless.

A similar, although much steeper, 20 minutes from the trailhead, on the *H. Newman Marsh Trail* will deposit your dog on top of 1,200-foot Observation Hill that earns its name with a trio of leafy overlooks. Marsh, incidentally was the man who developed the Jacob's Ladder Trail Scenic Byway, Route 20, that makes your drive to the park so memorable. Rather than taking these dueling attractions as separate out-and-back hikes you can link them with a comfortable four-mile loop, executed mostly on park roads.

The Civilian Conservation Corps (CCC) that developed the park in the 1930s also built Boulder Park, just east of the forest headquarters. Named for its high concentration of huge glacial erratics, it features a perfect leg-stretcher for your dog, an easy interpretive trail through a majestic stand of hemlocks.

69
West Barnstable Conservation Area

Barnstable County
West Barnstable; parking is on Farmersville Road north of Race Lane, 1.5 miles west of Route 149 and on Popple Bottom Road off Route 149.

This is one of the best places on Cape Cod to bring your dog for an extended, multi-hour adventure. More than 15 miles of narrow footpaths and dirt roads scramble across more than 1,100 acres north of the Cape Cod Airport. The forest is a multi-use destination with a shooting range, hunting (in season) and horse trails. The rugged terrain, long trails and hard-packed surfaces make this one of the most popular places on the Cape for mountain bikers. The named trails and mile markers are geared to the wheeled set but can also be used to plan your dog's hiking day, if it is going to be a long one. Glacial erratics help break up the long stretches of dense forest scenery and the many twists and turns and ups and downs keep the going lively. Dogs can trot under voice control here.

70
Douglas State Forest

Worcester County
Douglas; Cedar Street south of Route 16, five miles east of I-395, Exit 2.

This is a very popular park - on a great summer day you can expect it to actually fill up. But luckily for canine hikers none of those people are coming to use the trails. While the crush of humanity gathers around Wallum Lake, you can slip onto the 2.2-mile *Coffee House Loop* where your dog can enjoy a rushing stream, a cedar swamp, Aldrich Pond and trotting down the abandoned railbed of the Southern New England Trunkline. Or you can skip the crowds altogether and join the mountain bikers and horses on the old roads and trails north of Route 16 in the 5,730-acre park. Or better yet, come in the off-season and have the forest practically to yourselves and your dog can check out that beach on Wallum Lake she only heard stories of during the summer.

71
Robinson State Park

Hampden County
Agawam; on North Street off Route 187, north of Route 57

In 1908 John Cooley Robinson became the first president of Baystate Storage & Warehouse Co. in Springfield and built a warehouse regarded as one of the largest and best-equipped of its kind in the country. He retired four years later at the age of 47 to devote his time to the reclamation and development of the Agawam Meadows in West Springfield. In 1934 he donated 700 acres for what became the park named for his efforts.

Although Robinson State Park is scrunched in a narrow band along five miles of the Westfield River and is relatively urban, it sustains one of the most diverse woodlands in Massachusetts with over 50 native tree species. The finest stand of tulip poplars, the tallest tree in eastern forests, can be found here and that includes the state champion at 140 feet tall.

This is a busy place with activity on the water and along the paved road that hugs the river's edge. The best place to slip away with your dog on the paw-friendly sandy dirt and pine straw trails is in the eastern part of the park. There are many short, intersecting trail segments here so if you take a mis-step along the way you won't say off-course for long.

72
Estabrook Woods

Middlesex County
Concord; take Monument Street north of town and turn left on Liberty Street and right on Estabrook Street.

The most famous woods in Massachusetts, and maybe America, is Walden Pond where Henry David Thoreau went to live and espouse on the simple life. Your dog will never tramp the paths of Thoreau there - Walden Pond does not permit dogs.

But it many manys Walden Pond was not Thoreau's woods, it was Estabrook Woods. Walden was just a place he went to live for a couple of years and write about. The woods he called Estabrook Country was where his soul resided. His father operated a sawmill on one of the many tiny brooks that lubricate the land. Here the Thoreaus manufactured pencils from the cedars that grew in the forest. Pencil making was Henry's vocation throughout most of his adult life, he rediscovered the process to make a good pencil out of inferior graphite by using clay as the binder.

Thoreau's walks in Estabrook Woods are less famous than Walden since he wrote about them only in his journals. Even today, the woodlands are seldom visited. The 1200 acres are not a public park but is mostly part of Harvard's ecology study area. Other pieces of the land are owned by schools, private trusts and towns. Public access is permitted on most (not all) for low-impact traditional uses like hiking with your dog. Estabrook has defied development for two centuries and remains the rocky, rough and swampy land it was when Ralph Waldo Emerson referred to it as "the savage fertile houseless land."

73
Freedom Trail
Suffolk County
Boston Common; bounded by Beacon, Charles, Boylston, Tremont and Park streets.

A great hike with your dog doesn't have to take place on grass and dirt. The *Freedom Trail* winds through Boston for over two miles past 16 of the most nationally significant historic sites in America. Preserved and dedicated by the citizens of Boston in 1958, when the wrecking ball threatened, the red bricks lead to museums, churches, meeting houses, and burying grounds that tell the story of the American Revolution.

And it's not all pavement and curbstones for your dog. A logical starting point for your exploration of the *Freedom Trail* is the Boston Common. The Common is the oldest public park in the country, created in 1634 as a "cow pasture and training field." Cattle grazed here for 200 years, and could look up every now and then to see the occasional public hanging that took place in the Common. The park is about 50 acres in size and is the anchor for the Emerald Necklace, a system of connected parks that visit many of Boston's neighborhoods. Dogs are welcome on Boston Common and can even run off-leash from 5-7 a.m. and 5-7 p.m.

74
Crane Beach
Essex County
Ipswich; end of Argilla Road off Northgate Road, 1.5 miles from Route 133

Sometimes the greatest fortunes come from the most mundane products. In 1847, 15-year old Richard T. Crane learned the brass finishing trade as an apprentice in a Brooklyn foundry; a few years later he migrated west to Chicago and eventually built a 14-by-24 foot wooden shed where he manufactured couplings for lightning rod tips. For the first year he was the sole employee--molder, furnace tender, metal pourer, casting cleaner, and salesman. When his career ended more than a half-century later in 1912, Crane Co. was the world's largest manufacturer of valves and pipe fittings.

After the founder's death his son, Richard, Jr., became president and it was he who purchased what many consider to be New England's best beach at Castle Neck. He built an Italian Renaissance Revival villa atop Castle Hill, razed it in 1928 and replaced it with an even more magnificent 59-room Stuart-style mansion designed by architect David Adler. The Great House is the centerpiece of the Reservation that was established in 1949.

More than 1,200 acres of beachfront and dunes are covered with more than five miles of trails. Castle Neck is the site of the North Shore's largest maritime pitch pine forest. Dogs are allowed only from October 1 to March 31 and can walk only below the high tide line. Of course missing the summer season means your dog will miss the greenhead flies and you will miss the stiff parking fees.

75
Mount Grace State Forest
Franklin County
Warwick; on Route 78 north of town from Route 2A.

In 1676, Mary Rowlandson of Lancaster (a town 40 miles to the east) was captured, along with her infant daughter Grace, by a band of Wompanoag Indian warriors, led by King Phillip (see Redemption Rock, page 66). On a march toward Canada the baby died, and it is said to have been buried by her mother's hands at the foot of the mountain that now bears her name.

At 1,621 feet, Mount Grace is the third highest spot your dog can climb east of the Connecticut River in Massachusetts. And it will feel like it once you guide him away from the pine-scented, paw-friendly hiking trail and onto the rock-strewn Fire Tower Road to finish the one-mile journey to the summit. Once on top of Mount Grace there are no views from the clearing - until you climb one of the highest unfenced, unsupervised fire towers you are ever like to encounter. Your dog can climb the nine flights of wooden plank steps but the sides are unprotected and the landings small so she is better left tied to the ground.

The views from the lookout go a long way in every direction with the most conspicuous landmark being Mount Monadnock in New Hampshire. You can use the white-blazed *Metacomet-Monadnock Trail* in either direction to complete a loop down the mountain.

76
Nickerson State Park
Barnstable County
Brewster; on Route 6A, two miles from Exit 12 off Route 6 in Orleans.

Samuel Mayo Nickerson grew up on the Cape but left in 1847 to sell spirits to midwesterners in Chicago. He made his way from the distillery business into banking, earning millions along the way. After serving as president of the First National Bank of Chicago for 25 years, Nickerson returned to Brewster in 1890 and built a three-story, four-chimney home for his son, Roland. A stone tower was for gazing at the Atlantic. Fieldstone Hall sat on an 1,800-acre estate that included a carriage house, a windmill and tower used to generate electricity, and a private game preserve which is now Nickerson State Park.

Fieldstone Hall burned to the ground in 1906 taking the family's wardrobe, rare old china, and a myriad of paintings and books to ashes with it. The financial loss was tallied at $500,000 - $497,000 more than was covered by the Nickerson's insurance policy. Samuel Nickerson built a larger mansion - fireproof this time - on the ruins but Roland was not around to see it. Devastated by the conflagration he succumbed to poor health just two weeks after the disaster.

With a dog-friendly campground sporting over 400 sites, Nickerson is a good base for canine hikers to explore the Cape. It also makes it a very busy place. You could spend a weekend on the miles of paved trails and the 22-mile *Cape Cod Rail Trail* that passes through the park but the best place to take your dog is the hiking trails at the park ponds that are totally dependent on groundwater and precipitation. The best travels around Little Cliff Pond. Others visit Flax Pond and Cliff Pond. A hike to Higgins Pond will lead you to an excellent location to view endangered birds such as peregrine falcons and ospreys.

77
McLennan Reservation

Berkshire County

Tyringham; Fenn Road off Route 20, south of Tyringham center (park near the barn and walk up th edirt road to the trailhead on the left).

Robb de Peyster Tytus, a noted Egyptologist and politician, assembled a 1,000-acre estate from farms in Tyringham and Otis that he called Ashintully, from Gaelic meaning "on the brow of the hill." Between 1910 and 1912, Tytus built a 35-room Georgian-style mansion that would come to be known as the Marble Palace.

Tytus enjoyed his home for scarcely a year before dying in 1913. His widow Grace married John S. McLennan, a Canadian senator and newspaper publisher, a year later. The couple had one child, John Jr., who acquired the property in 1937. The Marble Palace burned to the ground in 1952, long after McLennan had established his residence in a farmhouse below. McLennan converted a nearby barn into a music studio, becoming an accomplished composer of piano and organ orchestral music and winning an American Academy of Arts and Letters music award. John McLennan donated 491 acres of his estate beginning in 1977 for this reservation.

This canine hike on the slopes of Round Mountain and Long Mountain is completely in the trees, about two miles including the walk up to the trailhead. You start out moving straight up but just as it appears you are in for a strenuous day the trail jogs left and levels out among Christmas ferns. When you reach old homestead stone walls the trail widens and becomes increasingly paw-friendly under towering hemlocks.

Soon you'll hear the sound of rushing water below and you begin to move beside an attractive, energetic stream. Now the remainder of the loop travels around the mountain. This remains a sporty outing for your dog but not the back-breaker it appeared when you took off on the trail. When Hale Pond is full it is one of the best doggie swimming pools in the Berkshires.

78
Rocky Woods Reservation
Norfolk County
Medfield; on hartford Road from Route 109, east of town and intersection with Route 27

There is a wonderful mix of canine hiking opportunities here: short nature walks and hours-long journeys to hilltops and scenic overlooks; ponds with sandy shores and footbridges; old quarries; modestly purchased views from hilltops; the remains of a pitchfork factory; country-lane walks and hayfield hikes; interesting woodlands; odd rock formations; and easy-to-follow marked trails.

Sounds like a great place to hike with your dog. And it is. But only dogs who are part of the Green Dogs program are welcome at Rocky Woods. Unless it is Sunday afternoon. Then you can bring your dog to these alluring trails from noon to closing.

79
Mount Misery
Middlesex County
Lincoln; located just off Route 117 (South Great Road), off Route 20 from I-95, Exit 26.

According to legend, a pair of yoked oxen wandered away from a nearby Colonial farm and got stuck on a tree, one on either side, with the yoke preventing them from moving forward. With a decided lack of teamwork there they remained, in misery, until they died. It certainly wasn't the climb up the 284-foot glacially carved hill that generated the name.

Mount Misery is part of the Lincoln Conservation Land, a 227-acre tract next to the Sudbury River that was preserved by the town in 1969. Your dog's reward for a hike here will be the pleasing pine-and-hemlock forest and occasional meadows, not the views, or rather lack of same, from the summit. The well-groomed, well-marked trails are a delight for any level of canine hiker.

80
Beartown State Forest
Berkshire County
Monterey; on Benedict Pond Road off Blue Hill Road from Route 23, 5.3 miles east of Route 7.

One legend holds that the park received its name from an early Lee pioneer who killed a bear here with a knotted rope. With more than 12,000 acres in Beartown State Forest there are plenty of multi-use to take off on with your dog - more than 30 miles worth. The unpaved roads and wide ski trails scoot around the forested hillsides and up mountains for a full day of canine hiking in the woods.

The star trail for dog owners will likely be the *Benedict Pond Loop*, a 1.5-mile jaunt around the 35-acre lake. The calming waters are in sight almost the entire trip. This is mostly level going, although it can get rocky under paw. The best stretch is on the opposite side of the water from the day-use areas where the trail slips along a ridge of hemlocks and rock formations.

The *Appalachian Trail* joins Benedict Pond at its eastern end and a short trip north leads to a jumble of rocks known as The Ledges. Further on, the trail explores the Swann State Forest and can be used for a canine hiking loop of several hours' duration.

81
South Mashpee Pine Barrens
Barnstable County
Mashpee; unpaved parking lot at Holland Mill Road (unmarked, opposite Old Dock Road), west of Great Neck Road, 1.8 miles south of Route 28 rotary.

Pine barrens can be an acquired taste - to some the endless acres of pitch pine with thick understories of scrub oak over dry, sandy terrain are a source of constant fascination. For others, a hike through pine barrens is a dreary slog where the view never changes. It doesn't help that some folks seem to equate the pitch pine forest, where the trees seldom climb above 50 feet and do appear scrubby in appearance, with a dumping ground. There is no need to poll your dog, however. She is likely to love romping on the paw-friendly sand roads.

What passes for a trail system here involves a ten-minute walk to a four-way intersection with Great Hay Road. This gives you an introduction to what hiking is like in the pine barrens (always best on a cool day as the sun can beat down on the miniature forest). If everyone is enthusiastic, continue on the nearly three-mile loop that lies straight ahead or to the left. To complete the full loop will require a short walk on the shoulder of an active paved roadway. Note also that near the beginning of the hike, the opening on your left is a Wampanoag Indian ceremonial area. The tribe has survived in this area for 10,000 years, helping the Pilgrims withstand their hardships when they landed in 1620. Respect the tribal traditions and stay on the trail through this private land.

As your dog explores, keep an eye out for the rare buck moth that lives only in barrens like these. The caterpillars gobble scrub oak leaves in May and June before burrowing underground in the heat of summer. Don't disturb the caterpillars - their spiny backs deliver a toxin similar to a bee sting. The buck moth emerges in mid-October, dressed in the white, black and orange colors f the season (and when the white-tailed buck was traditionally hunted, which is how they got their name. They mate furiously, lay their eggs back on the oak branches and die with the cold weather.

82
The Nature Trail and Cranberry Bog at Patriot Place
Norfolk County
Foxborough; on Route 1 behind the Bass Pro Shops.

A football stadium might not seem like the ideal place to hike with your dog but you won't want to overlook this nature trail. The half-mile loop is covered with paw-friendly wood chips the entire way around and splits its time between a cranberry bog, the last remaining active bog in the town of Foxborough, and a delightful piney forest. In the woodlands the rollercoaster trail bounds up small mounds that can get as steep as a 12% grade.

The trail around the bog, decorated by wildlife sculptures, is an interpretive one taking you through the lifecycle of the cranberry. The ripest berries are the ones with the most bounce, a characteristic learned in the 1880s by John "Pegleg" Webb who, due to his physical limitations, was unable to carry his stored berries down the stairs from the loft of his barn. To solve the problem, Webb simply poured the crop down the steps. He noticed that the firmest berries bounced to the bottom, while the bruised and unhealthy ones remained on the stairs. Because of this method, Webb was known for his high quality cranberries and able to demand top dollar in the market.

Completing the *Nature Trail* with your dog will take about the same amount of time as playing a quarter of football. And if it's not a good game, it is well worth going around again.

83
North Brook Cascades

Berkshire County

North Adams; at the end of Marion Avenue off Route 2, one mile from town center.

Less than a mile from the bustling center of downtown North Adams your dog will be a world away where Notch Brook squeezes down 40 feet with an appropriate roar. The Berkshire Natural Resources Council helped the city secure federal funding to acquire the Cascades in the 1970s.

If your dog has never been out beyond your neighborhood, this is an ideal trail to take that first hike. The *Cascades Trail* trips along and across the brook for an easy half-mile through a cool hemlock forest. There are just enough twists and rolls to provide the feel of a real woods trek with a satisfying payoff as you hear the plunging water well before you glimpse the Cascades dropping through the folds in the basaltic rocks. The pools below the falls are splendid venues for canine aquatics.

For more adventurous canine hikers the trail continues up the rocks to the top of the Cascades and continues down an old woods road that is actually an ancient extension of Marion Avenue. Come ready for bushwhacking if you plan an extended outing with your dog in these attractive woods.

A scenic walk through Notch Brook will reward a water-loving dog.

84
Questing

Berkshire County

New Marlborough; on New Marlborough Hill Road south of Route 57, five miles east on the intersection with Route 23.

The gifts of land that became the 438-acre Questing reservation, named for a mythical beast from King Arthur's Court, took place in the early 1990s. The flanks around Leffingwell Hill were settled back in the 1700s and the first non-Native American children were born here. After a century of struggling with the rocky soils all the farmers had migrated away and the settlement was abandoned.

Your dog's exploration of Questing begins with a long, gradual climb up a wide, old farm road. At the end you'll begin a loop that mixes a wide open field and a gorgeous woods walk through a hemlock forest. The 17-acre upland field of native meadow wildflowers attracts a variety of dragonflies and butterflies, including giant green darners and monarchs. The entire canine hike covers some two miles on Leffingwell Hill.

85
Goodwill Park

Plymouth County

Falmouth; on Gifford Street, south of Brick Kiln Road from Route 28

Joseph Story Fay was the first one of Falmouth's ummer residents, establishing a country retreat in the 1850s. He was a Bostonian who spent most of his year in Savannah, Georgia overseeing his family's cotton interests. In 1894, long before open space would become a critical resource, Fay gave Goodwill Park to the people of Falmouth. The name reflected his intent: it was a gesture of goodwill to the town.

The one thing for dogs to remember in Goodwill Park is that Grews Pond, the small one, is for swimming (off-season only) and Long Pond, the big one, is for looking. Long Pond and the town forest surrounding it make up the water supply area for Falmouth and access within 100 feet of the shoreline is prohibited. But your dog won't be in a hurry to leave the fat, paw-friendly dirt road that makes up the bulk of the five miles or so of rolling trails here. The park is home to a variety of tree species including red pine, white pine, hickory, beech, locust, oak, and Norway and red spruce; many are quite impressive.

86
Freetown-Fall River State Forest
Bristol County

Assonet; from South Main Street off Exit 10 of Route 24 turn left onto Route 79 north and right onto Elm Street which then turns into Slab Bridge Road and reaches the forest entrance in 1.5 miles.

The Commonwealth started acquiring land for this forest in the 1930s and twenty years later it had grown to over 5,000 acres. Canine hikers will target Freetown-Fall River for long, rambling outings but you will be sharing the multi-use trails with horses, mountain bikes and even motorcycles. Popular destinations include a quarry pond and mill pond connected by the *Long Trail* in the Rattlesnake Brook area. Scattered along the trail are more than 30 stone water holes constructed by the Civilian Conservation Corps in the early days of the park.

The one must-see destination in Freetown-Fall River is set apart from the main acreage in the northern end of the park: Profile Rock. The 50-foot outcropping suggested the profile of Chief Massasoit of the Wampanoags, whose reservation remains part of the forest today. There are two short hiking trails to view Profile Rock; one to its base and the other from atop a small hillock opposite the rock formation.

87
Woodsom Farm
Essex County

Amesbury; on Lion's Mouth Road (that was Friend Street), two miles west of town center and Route 150.

The town purchased the former dairy farm in 1989 to preserve open space and the 370-acre property has evolved into one of the best places for your dog to enjoy an open-field farm romp in Massachusetts. There is an easy hour's worth of hiking for your dog here and in adjacent Amesbury Town Forest on stacked loops of generous walking paths.loop, executed mostly on park roads. The Powow River, whose falls spawned the early growth of Amesbury, flows into the northwestern part of the park and makes a superb doggie swimming hole.

88
Jug End State Reservation

Berkshire County

Egremont; on Jug End Road off Mount Washington Road from Route 41 south of the village.

The name "Jug End" doesn't describe any physical features of this slice of 1,158 acres between the *Appalachian Trail* and the *Taconic Crest Trail* but rather derives from the German word "jugend" meaning "youth." During the Depression the valley was developed as a ski resort with hike-up and ski-down trails on Mt. Sterling to the west. The centerpiece of the resort, run by the Guilder Hollow Club, was an elaborate cattle barn that was constructed in 1928 and converted into a hotel.

In 1947 local residents came together to purchase the ski area and its popularity - as the closest Massachusetts slope to New York City - quickly led to the installation of two rope tows and, later, a 1,500-foot Mueller T-bar. In its heyday in the 1960s Jug End featured six trails with a vertical drop of 350 feet. The ski area closed in the early 1980s with the barn/hotel being abandoned and eventually torn down. The property has rapidly reverted to its natural state under the stewardship of the DCR and the Department of Fisheries and Wildlife.

The prime trail for canine hikers here is the *Jug End Loop Trail* that travels for two miles around the lowlands of Fenton Brook. There is just a minor elevation change as the path alternates between open fields and stands of northern hardwoods and open fields and Eastern Hemlock woodlands. Keep an eye out for your dog through the brushy fields where the path is studded with chopped stalks. Much of the time, however, all eyes will be on the surrounding hills.

The *Appalachian Trail* also passes through Jug End Reservation. You can access it by passing by the parking lot on Jug End Road to the unpaved section and a parking lot. About four miles to the south is Mount Everett.

89
Massasoit State Park

Bristol County
East Taunton; on Middleboro Avenue off South Street from Route 24, south off I-495.

This park lies on land once owned by Elizabeth Poole (sometimes spelled Pole) who came from Dorchester in 1637 and settled in "Titicutt," a section of the present East Taunton area. Legend maintains that she purchased her land, some 5,122 acres, from three Indians known as Josiah, David and Peter for "a jack-knife and a peck of beans."

The focus of Massasoit State Park is its campground that provides access to its four lakes. This makes it a busy place in season so you may want to schedule a visit with your dog after Columbus Day. A bonus this time of year is the sight of ripe cranberries bobbing in the bogs beneath dark green pine boughs.

Your dog will find sandy loam trails under paw and shady hiking throughout. This is flat, easy-going suitable for any dog. The trails aren't always marked but it is a small park so you won't stay lost for long if you wander down an unexpected path. And your dog will never be too far from a swim in one of the lakes.

90
Wompatuck State Park

Plymouth County
Hingham; on Free Street five miles north of Route 228 off Route 3.

Sachem Josiah Wompatuck was a member of the Massachuset tribe. His father was Chief Chickataubut. Wompatuck was exposed to Christianity at an early age and was considered a Praying Indian. He and members of the neighboring Wompanoag tribe transferred the land of present day Hingham to the town in 1665. During WWII the park was used as an ammunition depot by the United States military.

Dog owners are better served at adjacent and less-developed Whitney and Thayer Woods but Wompatuck is not without its charms for canine hikers. Once you get away from the campgrounds and paved biking paths you can hike for a long time and never see another soul in this big park, especially on weekdays. And your dog can go under voice control. No dogs in the centerpiece of the park, however - Mt. Blue Spring.

91
Old Jail Lane Conservation Area

Barnstable County
Barnstable; on Old Jail Lane, south of Route 6A and west of Hyannis Road.

If your Cape Cod dog finds the mountain bikes and horses on the extensive West Barnstable Conservation Area trail (page 127) troublesome, try the trails in this 180-acre park in the shadow of the Mid-Cape Highway. Your dog will love the rollercoaster feel of the trails bounding to the top of the next rise to see what awaits on the other side. It was glaciers scraping and gouging the land 15,000 years ago that shaped the steep ridges and sandy depressions here.

There are a quartet of trails at Old Jail Lane that offer a variety of canine hiking loops, well-marked with mapboards at key junctions. No great destinations are here for your dog, no swimming holes and the overlook will reveal just another view of the oaks and pines; just an hour well spent in the salt air. Well-behaved dogs can go under voice control and the old roads and paths get such limited use that the wispy grasses on the trail may grow high enough to tickle your dog's tummy.

92
Boxford State Forest

Essex County
Topsfield; from Exit 51 of I-95 take Endicott Road west to Middleton Road and turn right to forest on the left.

If your dog isn't particular about groomed trails, doesn't need any facilities and won't mind the occasional flooded trail then a trip to Boxford State Forest is in order. A mishmash of state and locally-owned properties have created a huge unbroken chunk of over 2000 acres west of Topsfield.

Your reward for these minor inconveniences is almost guaranteed solitude for most of your time in this richly diverse woodland featuring hemlock and hardwoods and acres of red maple swamp. If your dog is hankering for a destination hike set course for Bald Hill, the highest natural point in Boxford at an elevation of 243 feet. Hunting is permitted in the fall in much of the forest.

93
Brooks Woodland Preserve
Worcester County
Petersham; on East Street, .8 mile east of Route 32

OK, there are a few problems here. Trail maintenance is spotty, the maze of trails is poorly marked and confusing and the parking lot is nowhere near the best trails. But if your dog can get past these, there are more than 13 miles of lightly used, easy-to-trot trails that she is likely to love.

Part of the problem is the awkward lay of the land - James Wilson Brooks bought 70 parcels during his lifetime that would become the bulk of the Preserve's 558 acres. Born in Petersham in 1833, Brooks earned degrees from Brown University and Harvard Law School and served as American Vice Consul in Paris during the Civil War. He engaged in some colorful entrepreneurial activities out west, and finally parlayed a small manufacturing venture into the highly lucrative and powerful United Shoe Machinery Company.

As it is configured today, the Preserve features three main tracts running on a north-south axis. You should seek out the largest, the central Swift River Tract. Some highlights include scenic vistas, remnants of homesteads and farms, open meadows and interesting geological features such as the "Indian Grinding Stones," frost-fractured boulders said to have been used by Nipmuc Indians to pummel corn with stone pestals in the faint depressions. Most of the trails here are old farm roads and it is best to confine your canine hiking day on these after recent rains.

94
Harold Parker State Forest
Essex County
North Andover, 1951 Turnpike Road off Exit 41 from I-93.

There are more than 30 miles of old logging roads and somewhat rough trails for your dog to trot along in the more than 3,000 acres of this state forest. There are also several ponds for a refreshing doggie dip.

But the real attraction of Harold Parker State Forest for dog owners is a superior campground with roomy sites right in Boston's backyard. It is probably the closest tail-friendly campground to the city, certainly from the north side.

95
Bay Farm Conservation Area

Plymouth County

Duxbury, Kingston; south of Route 3A, east of Route 3, Exit 10. Turn down Park Street and bear left on Loring/Bay Landing Road to parking lot on left.

The landowners of the Plymouth Bay Colony began to clear this picturesque land by the Kingston Bay in 1627. After three centuries the Bay Farm Company was established to combine several of the tracts into an expansive dairy farming operation that pioneered the production of milk in a "clean, pure way." Upwards of four-score cows grazed here until the mid 1950s when the Duxbury Playhouse staged community productions in the former barn and outbuildings. The land began to be conserved in the 1960s and today some 80 acres have been set aside for recreation, only a sliver of the total farm that once was.

The trail system at Bay Farm trips through open pastureland festooned with wildflowers and exuberant grasses. Half of the farm is mowed each year but the strip of hills bedside the bay has regenerated into woodland. Of particular interest is a grove of cedars at the crest of a small hill straight out from the parking lot. In addition to romping through the avenues cut into the fields your dog will love a small sandy-muddy-grassy (depending on the tide) beach on Kingston Bay. Bay Farm is also the southern terminus of the *Bay Circuit Trail*, the 200-mile long greenbelt ringing Boston from the north shore to the south shore.

96
Mill Pond

Essex County

West Newbury; south of town on Main Street (Route 113)

Mill Pond and Pipestave Hill offer more than 200 acres of multi-length trails in rolling hills and cleared pastureland. The trails, some marked and some not, range from wide thoroughfares to single file passages on boardwalk. Longer expeditions can reach all the way to the Merrimac River.

These are popular trails for hiking, horseback riding and cross-country skiing. It is also very popular with dog owners, so much so it may threaten their welcome. If you stop by follow the lead of the locals regarding leashed areas and swimming in the oh-so-alluring pond with its easy shore access.

97
Berlin Road Trail System

Berkshire County

Clarksburg; on Berlin Road from Torrey Woods road off Route 2 after the road diverges from Route 7.

Most of the property on Berlin Mountain, whose summit actually rests just across the state line in New York, was in the hands of many small landowners. This mitigated against development on the steep slopes.

In 1933 members of the Williams Outing Club laid out a trail to the 2,798-foot summit and in 1960 Ralph Townsend, the Williams College ski coach for 22 years, purchased a bit of Berlin Mountain and developed it into a new ski area for the college, complete with 30- and 40- meter natural jumps and a giant slalom run. In the early 1980s, a paucity of snow and a lack of snowmaking capabilities made it difficult for the ski team to continue to practice at Berlin and the site was abandoned.

In 1998, under the stewardship of the Williamstown Rural Lands Foundation (WRLF), new loop trails were built at the end of Berlin Road, including educational signs. You can come to Berlin for an easy, relaxed outing with your dog or a tail-dragging workout. The WRLF trail is on paw-friendly terrain as it rolls mildly   to a scenic overlook and joins a logging road, crosses the brook and then climbs to an old ski area at the top of Berlin Road. The gravel road closes your loop to the trailhead. The *Waterfall Trail* is a short spur off the first part of the trail, leading to a narrow ribbon of cascading water.

The entrance to the *Class of '33 Trail* is 100 yards to the east of the parking area. This path to the summit can be rough going and maintenance spotty at times. In addition, logging activities have muddled the route. Of the several alternate routes up Berlin Mountain, where your reward is 360-degree views into New York and back to Massachusetts, the approach from Petersburg Pass, where the *Taconic Crest Trail* crosses Rt 2, offers the least elevation change - less than 600 feet. The trail skirts the side of Mount Raimer, then descends to Berlin Pass before climbing up to Berlin Mountain. Distance one way is 2.7 miles.

98
Copicut Woods

Bristol County
Fall River; Indian Town Road from Blossom Road off Old Bedford Road from Exit 9 off I-195.

Although less than 15 minutes from downtown Fall River, Copicut Woods can seem as remote a woods walk as anywhere in Massachusetts. The property is the southern gateway to the 13,600-acre Southeastern Massachusetts Biore-serve, which includes state-owned forest and wildlife management areas and the wooded landscape protecting the city's drinking water supply.

After bouncing down dirt roads and crashing through barely maintained trails your dog may question your wisdom in coming to the undeveloped 516-acre Copicut Woods. All doubts will flow away once you reach the mile-long Miller Lane and step back into the 1800s (except for the trees) to stroll down a magnificent cart path. In places a Great Dane won't be able to see over the impressive stone walls that line the road.

Miller Lane leads to the stone ruins of the Isaac Miller Homestead, founda-tions with stone steps scattered in a clearing. At the opposite end of the cart path is a rare dry tunnel - a narrow stone underpass that enabled livestock to move between fields.

The stone walls along Miller Lane in Copicut Woods are as impressive as your dog is likely to find in Massachusetts.

99
Agassiz Rock

Essex County
Manchester-by-the-Sea; north of Route 128. Take Exit 15 onto School Street north for a half-mile to a small parking area on the right.

There are actually two Agassiz Rocks, a Big and a Little. The site is named for the 19th century professor of natural history, Louis Aggasiz. He was the one who first explained the presence of the massive granite boulders that are scattered across the New England landscape. Most people in the 1800s thought the big rocks were leftovers from the Great Flood - the one Noah was in. Aggasiz theorized that the rocks, called "erratics," were instead scraped up and left behind by retreating glaciers. The site was named by Essex Institute students in 1874, a year after Aggasiz died. The great man is reported to have come out from Harvard to visit the boulders to help advance his theory.

Today a moderate, completely wooded, one-mile balloon footpath visits the Agassiz rocks. The more arresting of the two is actually Little Aggassiz Rock that is perched atop Beaverdam Hill. Big Aggasiz Rock is encountered in a shrub swamp, somewhat obscured by its vegetative surroundings. No one, in fact, knows how deep into the ground Big Aggasiz Rock is embedded in the muck.

100
Clarksburg State Park

Berkshire County
Clarksburg; on Middle Road off Route 8, three miles north of Route 2.

The founding fathers of Clarksburg were Captain Matthew Ketchum, Colonel William Bullock and Nicholas Clark, with the town taking the name of the last in 1769. Not much of a workout for your dog on the 368 acres around this pretty, landscaped lake-central park. There are almost ten miles of foot trails in Clarksburg State Park with the star canine hike being the 3-mile *Pond Loop Trail* that actually doesn't spend much time near the water. Your dog will need to navigate through the developed day-use area to return to your starting point on this journey. You will get those scenic water views by closing the circuit on the *Shoreline Trail*. Another short trail to enjoy is the *Blueberry Trail* that loops near the beach area. Additional trails radiate away from the Pond Loop for more hiking with your dog but these will dead-end at the park boundaries.

Index to Tail-Friendly
Parks in
Massachusetts...

3516058

Made in the USA